# The Eye of Fire

# The Eye
# of Fire

Graham Phillips

Martin Keatman

SAFFRON WALDEN
THE C.W. DANIEL COMPANY LIMITED

First published in Great Britain in 1986 by
The C. W. Daniel Company Limited
1 Church Path, Saffron Walden,
Essex, England

ISBN 85207 172 8

Set in 10/11pt Melior and printed by Hillman Printers (Frome) Ltd
Frome, Somerset, England

To Victoria

# Contents

Chapter                                                    Page

Author's Note                                                9

The Green Stone                                             11

One            Visions through Time                         15
Two            The Dark Watcher                             25
Three          An Unknown Legacy                            33
Four           The Living Dead                              43
Five           The Secret                                   61
Six            The Cave                                     73
Seven          The Summoning                                79
Eight          Nightmare                                    85
Nine           Something in the House                       93
Ten            Psychic Fury                                 99
Eleven         Haunted                                     107
Twelve         The Seance                                  113
Thirteen       The Last Hope                               121
Fourteen       The Nightcomer                              127
Fifteen        The Voyage                                  133
Sixteen        The Eye of Fire                             145
Seventeen      Lady of Light                               159

# Author's Note

Unfortunately, this book is true.

# The Green Stone

In October 1979, a number of men, women and children throughout Great Britain independently received a strange psychic message, a clue to enable them to discover the secret hiding place of a priceless buried treasure, a green gem-stone fashioned in Ancient Egypt and lost from the pages of history for untold centuries. In legend the stone was believed to hold awesome supernatural power. Drawn together by the message, this group of ordinary British people were catapulted onto a terrifying search, a race against time to find the hidden jewel.

In September 1979, Graham Phillips and Martin Keatman were working for a magazine called **Strange Phenomena**, when they were contacted by Mrs. Marion Sunderland, a housewife and mother of five living in Clwyd, North Wales. She and her twelve year old daughter Gaynor had received a psychic message telling them they must embark on a search for a lost jewel.

They were not alone in making this extraordinary claim. Others, too, contacted Phillips and Keatman at their Wolverhampton headquarters and reported identical psychic impressions. Incredibly, they were all unknown to one another and came from different towns and cities throughout Britain. Still more amazingly, Graham and two other researchers involved in the investigation also started to receive parts of the message. These were Terry Shotton, a safety officer with Staffordshire County Council, and Alan Beard, a Marketing Engineer for the G.P.O. Together with Graham and Martin they began to solve the mystery.

All the impressions pieced together to form a clear psychic message. The essence of it was that the Megalithic peoples who once inhabited the British Isles over three thousand years ago, the people who built Stonehenge, had made a fantastic discovery: the secret of awakening the innermost psychic power of the human mind. However, this knowledge was misused and brought about their downfall when it fell into the hands of barbarian warlords. The country was ravaged by warfare and slid back into a dark age of chaos. The vanquished Megalithic priesthood travelled south and arrived eventually in Ancient Egypt. There they created a powerful talisman, a green stone that held the means to overcome the destructive power now wielded by the treachorous rulers of their homeland.

Many years later their descendants returned to the British Isles and, led by a great warrior queen, Gwevaraugh, defeated the last of those who had misused the ancient knowledge. From then onwards the secret was known only to those few who handed the stone down from one generation to the next, until it came into the possession of a medieval society called The Order of Meonia. In the early seventeenth century some of those belonging to this mystical fraternity were English catholics persecuted during the reign of James I, and who consequently became involved in the Gunpowder Plot of 1605. After the discovery of Guy Fawkes, about to ignite the barrels of gunpowder beneath the House of Lords, The Green Stone was quickly hidden in a secret location and was lost from the pages of history.

The message was incredible. But however unbelievable it was, they felt compelled to investigate further. Guided by new psychic impressions and historical research they arrived at Harvington Hall, an Elizabethan manor-house in the heart of Worcestershire, where they discovered a series of paintings, made in the early seventeenth century, containing a secret coded message.

On deciphering the message they were led to a secluded spot in Worcestershire near the village of Severn Stoke. Here, in the foundations of an old stone footbridge overlooking a stretch of water called Knight's Pool, they discovered a short sword bearing the coat of arms of Mary Queen of Scots.

A week after this remarkable find Gaynor phoned the authors to say that she had received another psychic impression. If she held the sword she claimed she would be able to locate the Stone, which was buried in a casket near the bridge. At almost precisely the same time, and completely independently of Gaynor's call, both Terry Shotton and Alan Beard had strong psychic impressions of the stone in a heavy metal casket hidden beneath the ground.

On the morning of Monday 29 October, 1979, Gaynor was taken to the bridge, and using the sword as a divining rod she eventually directed them to a large meander on the River Avon called the Swan's Neck. Further research and psychic impressions finally led them to the precise hiding place, and the following day a heavy brass casket was unearthed from a grassy mound on the banks of the river. Inside was the Green Stone.

This startling historical discovery was only the beginning. After many months of painstaking research they discovered that The

Order of Meonia had not disbanded following the loss of the Stone after the Gunpowder Plot, but had continued until the late nineteenth century. However, in 1875, the leader of the Order, a wealthy heiress called Mary Heath, and the eight other members, disappeared following a confrontation with the mysterious occultist John Laing in the Midland town of Wolverhampton.

* * * *

Try as they might to absorb themselves in the rigours of everyday life, many of those who had found themselves involved in these extraordinary events still wanted to know what really lay behind their fantastic experiences. Two years after discovering the Green Stone the most important questions still remained unanswered. What had become of the strange secret once held by the Order of Meonia? What terrible event brought about its downfall at the end of the last century? And how were they themselves involved?

The answers to these questions were more disturbing and more frightening than any of them could possibly have imagined. Their year long search became a real-life horror story, a nightmarish race against time to seek The Eye of Fire and discover it's terrible secret.

# Chapter One
# Visions through Time

**March 1982**

During the late winter of 1982, with the Green Stone safely stored in the vaults of a Welsh bank, Terry Shotton, Martin Keatman and Graham Phillips decided to conduct a thorough investigation into the events surrounding the final days of the Order of Meonia, but by March all their lines of inquiry had been exhausted. They were no nearer to solving the mystery. A thorough historical investigation had proved fruitless, and if written records concerning the Order of Meonia after 1875 did exist, the group had been unable to discover them. They had approached many of the country's leading authorities on the occult, but when questioned they either knew nothing or preferred to remain silent about the illusive Order. Biddulph Grange, once the Staffordshire home of Mary Heath, the last leader of the Order, is now an orthopaedic hospital, and it was impossible for anything new to be discovered there. The living descendants of some of those people named among the nineteenth century Order were interviewed, but with the same result. Some knew of the mysterious disappearance of their ancestors, but were unable to give further information. No-one seemed to know anything new about the Order of Meonia.

They now felt that if they were ever to unravel the mystery they must have a new lead. Only one line of investigation remained, a controlled attempt to obtain information by psychic means. In the past, members of the group had received psychic impressions that had proved invaluable, so perhaps they could do it again. The problem was, however, that on previous occasions the psychic impressions had been unprompted, usually received only by individuals. The chances of awakening paranormal abilities on demand, not to mention focussing them onto a particular subject, seemed highly unlikely. But they considered it was worth a try. However they all felt if the experiment failed their quest to solve the mystery would probably have to be abandoned.

The question was, which of them would make the attempt? Marion Sunderland and her daughter, Gaynor, had been the most accurate psychics, and so they volunteered.

On 20th March they decided to hold a meeting at Graham's house in Coventry. So, just before 8.00 p.m. that Saturday evening nine people sat around the large oak table in the living room. Marion and Gaynor sat next to Martin who was to record all that took place. Graham and Terry were also present, with a number of disinterested witnesses, so that if any paranormal phenomena did occur it could be independently verified. The first of these was Mary Harrison, a Coventry school teacher. Out of curiosity she had attended a series of lectures given by Graham and Martin in Coventry and was intrigued by their experiences, so she asked if she could attend a group meeting to form an opinion for herself. Second was Jean Smith, a local Council employee they had also met at a lecture series, and finally David and Sheila Bavington, a self employed couple from Warwickshire. Everyone had paper and a pen with which to make notes.

The time was now 8.12 p.m., and as an aid to concentration Terry turned off the lights, so the room was dark except for a solitary candle in the middle of the table. Everyone sat quietly, their emotions a combination of excitement and anticipation.

Somewhere in the distance a car rumbled past, a droning echo far away. A young couple walked by outside, their raised voices briefly penetrating the strange silence of the darkened room. Even these familiar evening sounds receded into the night as time went by and the darkness closed in about them.

As the candle flickered and time passed, the tension began to mount and an uncanny stillness descended on the house. All eyes fell on Marion and Gaynor sitting at the head of the table, their features slightly distorted by the constantly moving shadows of the candle flame. Around them loomed nine huge figures, their eerie shadows swaying and dancing on the walls.

It was at 8.35 p.m. that Marion spoke, her voice apprehensive.

'I can see a tree,' she began, concentrating on the image in her mind's eye. 'It's been dead for many years.' She fell silent, and Martin scribbled down her words in the half-light. At the far side of the table Mary opened her mouth to say something, but Marion spoke again.

'I'm sure something happened at this place many years ago, something we must know about.' She continued, describing a fresh image that was forming. 'Yes, I can see a young woman in Victorian clothes.'

'Do you know where she is? Can you describe it?' Graham whispered.

Marion shook her head slowly. 'I don't know, it's probably just my imagination.'

'I don't think so,' a woman's voice suddenly broke in. It was Mary Harrison. 'I don't know how but I can see it too.'

'I'm deadly serious, I can see it too' she added when no-one answered.

Graham was about to ask her at what point the image had formed when something else unexpectedly happened.

'I can see it,' said Sheila Bavington quietly, 'I can see it very clearly.'

Encouraged by these confirmations Marion continued to describe what she could see. 'The oak tree is in the grounds of a large old house, possible a mansion.'

'I think it's a castle,' said Sheila. 'There's a moat and a portcullis.' To their increasing amazement David Bavington spoke next.

'I feel a bit daft saying this, but I can see a shield with six daggers on it, carved in stone, high up on a large old building.'

Graham, Martin and Terry stared at each other in numbed silence, astounded at what was happening. It seemed unlikely that Mary, Sheila and David were really experiencing these images yet surely they would not say so just for effect. They had no choice but to let things run their course and make a judgement later.

Quite suddenly everyone began speaking at once, Martin scribbled frantically.

'I can see a woman and what looks like a privet maze,' said Mary.

'And a bronze statue of two lovers protruding from a lake next to the building,' said David.

'Don't ask me why,' said Jean 'but I can see rows of privet bushes fashioned like guardsmen's helmets.'

* * * *

Although still quite young, her haggard expression belonged to a much older woman. Riding side-saddle on a jet black horse she cantered along a broad driveway toward the manor-house. Her cape billowed in the gusting wind as overhead the skies darkened with each passing minute.

Gaynor looked on and listened as the shrill clatter of the horse's hooves echoed hollowly on the cobbled forecourt.

The woman dismounted and drew her cape tightly about her. A stableboy took the horse's reins as she commanded him to

**wait, and with a last anxious glance back along the driveway she turned and hurried into the building.**

* * * *

The sound of David's voice drifted into Gaynor's mind as the vision slowly faded.

'It's a cellar,' he said thoughtfully, 'The woman is going down a flight of steps into a stone vaulted cellar.' He quickly sketched what he had seen and added emphatically, 'She's looking for something.'

Jean stared intently at David's drawing. 'That's almost exactly what I've just seen.' she said

Graham shook his head in amazement. 'Me too,' he said, pushing forward his own drawing.

Gaynor was only partly aware of the conversation as she once again passed into the vision.

* * * *

**She was hurriedly climbing the steps and leaving the cold damp cellar. Emerging into the harsh daylight of the forecourt she felt cold water against her cheeks. From the black scudding clouds a heavy rain had begun to fall. The stableboy stood quietly tending the horse, whispering to it and stroking its mane as it stirred at the sight of the woman. With hasty, courteous thanks she took the reins and mounted. In seconds she was gone, swiftly and skilfully turning the horse and galloping away from the manor.**

**Gaynor could almost feel as the woman must have felt. Cold rain driving into her anguished face, soaking her long fair hair. The smell of sweat, saddle soap and the dripping horse's mane as she passed along the narrow roadway, wide open parkland to either side. She wished to ride with even greater speed but knew she could not. Care was essential with the distance she had yet to travel. Still the black rain drove down upon her, drenching her cape and body. Occasionally she turned and looked back through the mist of rain over the way she had come. She hoped above all that she was not being pursued. But her hope was forlorn. It would only be a matter of time.**

* * * *

A warm hand gently took hold of Gaynor's left arm. She stirred and half opened her eyes finding herself back in the candle-lit room.

'Are you all right?' whispered Terry. Gaynor smiled and nodded, turning to her mother who placed a reassuring arm around her shoulders.

'Are you all right?' Marion said softly.

Gaynor nodded and looked at the others seated in the half light around the table. They had fallen silent and were looking concernedly towards her. Someone spoke, but the voice faded as again she returned to the vision.

\* \* \* \*

She was still riding, still glancing nervously behind her, but now the scene had changed. The road had widened and was bordered by irregular hedgerows. To her left stood a church at the foot of a small rounded hill, the only outstanding feature on the otherwise flat terrain.

Again the scene changed. The rain still fell on the woman who was now soaked to the skin. The horse whinnied and snorted as she dismounted. She had stopped beside a high stone tower, something like a church but stripped of its adjoining chapel. With a final look about her she opened a small leather purse strapped to her waist and carefully took something from it. She unclenched her rain spattered hand and Gaynor saw the object on the woman's outstretched palm. A small elliptical stone, a beautiful red-orange that seemed almost transluscent on her skin. The woman sighed, clenched her fist and entered the tower.

Once again the scene changed, only this time the sensation was different, as Gaynor was somehow removed from the vision. The intimate bond she had shared with the troubled woman was severed, leaving her an innocent bystander, invisibly witnessing an event that she now knew had taken place over a century ago.

The woman galloped down the long straight road, splashing desperately through the deep pools of rain water gathering on the uneven surface. Gaynor sensed the woman's anguish, the tense knot in her stomach as she looked behind her. Fear coursed through her body as she caught sight of three men moving towards her in the rain. She was being pursued by three cloaked figures on horseback. Turning her horse from the road she raced across the open countryside, the water-logged fields holding back her steed. Still the downpour cascaded in sheets onto the sodden landscape. Broken fences and flooded ditches flashed by as the horse raced still faster. She was far from her destination, alone and uncertain. The men gained on her, drawing even closer.

As she jumped a fallen tree trunk the horse twisted and fell. She was thrown violently into the air as the animal crashed to the ground rolling painfully over her. It scrambled awkwardly back onto its legs, taking a few faltering steps to stand protectively over its mistress. But the broken body of the woman lay motionless on the ground.

The three men reached her, dismounted and gathered round the lifeless form. A tall bearded figure knelt and turned the woman onto her back. Gaynor could not distinguish his features, but something about him made her feel uneasy. An ice cold chill tingled through her as she sensed the aura of darkness spilling from him.

As she slowly opened her eyes to the familiar surroundings of the room Gaynor knew she had witnessed the woman's death.

* * * *

The group sat quietly listening in the flickering candlelight as Gaynor recounted the details of her vision. Mary was the first to speak. 'The hill you mentioned with the church next to it, did it look something like this?' She pushed a drawing across the table to Gaynor. It depicted a round hill topped with two trees. Before Gaynor could answer, Martin, Graham and David began talking excitedly, each holding out their own drawings.

It was incredible, for all their independently made sketches were virtually identical. The round hill was in all of them, as were the leafless trees on top. Mary and Martin had drawn two trees, David and Graham three. Martin, David and Graham had sketched in a church to the left of the hill, and Mary and Martin had written 'Moat' at the bottom.

They had made almost identical drawings. It was astounding. As Gaynor had been 'asleep' Terry and Marion had gestured for the group to remain silent, assuming that she was perhaps experiencing a vision. This had occured on previous occasions, but never before when others had been present. During this time Mary, Graham, Martin and David had all, unknown to one another, made their drawings. Graham and David had experienced a lucid colour image in their mind's eye, while Mary and Martin had felt compelled to draw almost automatically. In addition, Jean told them that she too had experienced a vivid mental impression of a very similar place. All of these impressions had occured as Gaynor experienced her vision, well before she told them about it.

The similarity of the impressions astounded everyone. Nearly all those present had experienced some form of psychic impression. And most amazing of all, they had also been experienced by the disinterested observers. It now seemed possible that in some way they had all shared a vision through time.

'If something is hidden in that tower we ought to try and find it,' said Graham. 'Have your any idea where it is Gaynor?'

'I'm afraid not,' she answered.

'The woman rode along the Fosse Way,' interrupted Sheila, 'it's an old Roman road. That's where she fell.'

'What makes you so sure?' asked Martin.

'I honestly don't know,' said Sheila, 'but I'm certain it's the Fosse Way.'

'Wait a moment,' said Mary, 'I've seen this place before.' She was examining her drawing of the hill.

'I know where I've seen that statue,' exclaimed David suddenly, 'At Coombe Abbey.'

'Where's that?' asked Martin.

'About six miles east of Coventry.'

Jean and Mary were quick to agree, explaining that Coombe Abbey is a local Coventry beauty spot, the Abbey itself is closed but it's gardens are open to the public all the year round.

They wondered if the old house really was Coombe Abbey, and if it wasn't more than just coincidence that they happened to be in Coventry. On more than one previous occasion in the past they had been led to the right area to discover what they needed to find. The possibility that David might be correct was strengthened when Mary suddenly recalled where she had previously seen the hill.

'It's Brinklow Hill,' she said, 'it's only a couple of miles from Coombe Abbey. And if Mrs Bavington is right about the woman riding down the Fosse Way then I really think you may be on to something. The Fosse Way runs right past Brinklow Hill.'

As they pieced the information together it was becoming increasingly apparent that the visions were accurate. Still the most astounding fact though, was how their observers had become involved in the visions. By fate or coincidence it was fortunate they were involved, because not being locals to Coventry the others would never have identified the locations in the visions.

'So when did it all take place and who was the woman?' asked Terry.

Gaynor said she was sure the year had been 1865, the year Mary Heath had become the leader of the Order of Meonia. She added that Mary had inherited the position after the untimely death of the woman in the vision, who was the previous leader of the Order, but she did not know the woman's name.

'And the men,' continued Terry, 'who were they?'

Gaynor shook her head. 'I've no idea.'

'I think we can identify one of them,' offered Graham. 'John Laing. Since he brought about the downfall of the Order in 1875, we can only suppose he was working against them ten years before.'

Terry agreed.

Now they had to work out what it all meant, particularly what the Red Stone was that had apparently been hidden in the tower by the woman. As far as they knew there had been only one such item associated with the Order, the Green Stone which they had already been led to find. So did a second Stone exist?

They wondered if they had succeeded in discovering a new lead about the Order of Meonia and possibly even the secret it possessed. If this was so, they were puzzled why they had received psychic impressions of a time some ten years before the Order was destroyed in 1875. If Gaynor was right about the date, then perhaps, fascinating as it was, this information was valueless.

The four invited guests found the entire episode particularly strange, and a far cry from what they had expected. For the original group members there were mixed emotions. If there was a second Stone they were being directed to rediscover, a Stone that perhaps held the key to the inner secret of the Order of Meonia, they might well be thrown headlong onto a new search.

As they talked on into the late evening none of them had any way of knowing where the vision might lead.

In the safety of the candle-lit room the prospect of discovering this strange secret was engaging and exciting. But it was only moments before they were reminded of the darker side of such a quest.

* * * *

Sheila Bavington was bewildered. For the first time in her life she had witnessed something she could not explain. She was uncertain of what had happened or how such things could occur. She found it difficult to believe they had all really shared parts of the same vision. There was no point in trying to work it out now. For the time being the evening's events were over and she would try to remain as open-minded as possible.

But for Sheila the night was not over. Something unseen entered the house and every nerve of her body sensed its presence in the room. It was like a shocking blast of wintry air sending an icy shiver down her spine.

Then before she had a chance to utter a word she saw it. In the deep shadows at the far corner of the room something moved. Sheila blinked hard, surely it was her imagination or an optical illusion. She looked again. Her chest tightened with fear and her heart began to pound. By the half light of the flickering candle a dark, nebulous shape was taking form. Dumbstruck and paralysed with fear she watched the macabre materialisation taking place before her very eyes. There he was, as clear as day, out of nowhere, the unmistakable figure of a man. A tall bearded man dressed entirely in black, fixing her eyes with a cold hypnotic glare.

The seconds seemed like hours as she stared transfixed in horror, unable to move or speak. Then, with a desperate effort, she gasped aloud and shouted to the others in the room. But as her terrified cry pierced the night, the shadowy image melted silently away into the darkness.

## Chapter Two
# The Dark Watcher

It was difficult to know if Sheila Bavington had really seen something in the corner of the darkened room, something that vanished before anyone else had time to see it.

They had to consider that it could have been a strange effect of the candle light, a dark shadow coincidentally formed into the shape of a man. However, Sheila was positive about what she had seen.

Before they went their separate ways that evening they arranged to meet the following day. Certainly a trip to Coombe Abbey and Brinklow Hill would confirm or deny the accuracy of the visions.

The Sunday morning of March 21 dawned mild and dry. For the hundreds of local people who visited Coombe Abbey that day it was like any other Sunday, a welcome break from the routine of nine to five work and a chance to be with family and friends. But for the small group drawn together by recent events, Coombe Abbey held more than the attraction of a local beauty spot, as it was possibly linked with their search to discover the secret of the Order of Meonia.

By 10.30 a.m. all but Terry had arrived. And as they sat drinking tea and coffee in Graham's front room Gaynor made an unexpected announcement.

'I have a feeling that we must go to Knight's Pool immediately.'

Knight's Pool was the secluded stretch of water where two and a half years before Graham and Andy Collins had discovered a sword in the foundations of an old bridge at one end of the lake. This sword had led them to the Green Stone.

'Knight's Pool, why?' asked Marion.

'I just know it's important,' Gaynor replied cautiously. 'There's something there we must see.'

However Terry had still not arrived and a few minutes later he telephoned to say he had been delayed and could not make it until after lunch.

So they decided to drive over to Coombe Abbey and Brinklow Hill as planned, and meet Terry back in Coventry later on. A visit to Knight's Pool would have to wait until the afternoon. Gaynor was not pleased at the delay.

Marion then mentioned that before Gaynor had spoken of Knight's Pool she had quite suddenly received a strong mental image of Andy Collins. Since Andy moved to London in 1982 she had not seen him, so it seemed strange that he should come into her mind out of the blue. The reason, however, only became clear later that day.

Shortly after 11.00 a.m. that bright Sunday morning the group left Coventry. The road wound eastwards for six miles before they got their first view of Coombe Abbey. They all felt a mixture of excitement and apprehension as they drove the quarter of a mile up the avenue of tall, evenly spaced lime trees leading to the monastic building. Leaving the main road it was as if they had driven into a Gainsborough scene. Ahead, the broad straight driveway, and to either side the majestic trees rising high above, then before them stood the stark grey manor-house, dramatically outlined against the clear morning sky.

'Look,' said Marion, pointing to the solitary, lifeless oak tree standing beside the road. 'That's exactly what I saw last night, I'm sure its the right place.'

Gaynor peered out of the window as they turned into the visitors car park. She was still not sure. The woman she saw in her vision had not ridden through the main gate so if this was the place she had taken a different route.

As they walked from the car park across the grass towards the Abbey buildings, all around them young children were running to and fro in the bright morning sun. Everything seemed quite normal, but it was only moments later that they discovered another indication that they were indeed in the right place. An old stone footbridge led across the deep moat onto a cobbled forecourt. Leaning over the stone parapet to obtain a better view they noticed a heavy wooden portcullis in the Abbey wall down at water level. Here the moat seemed to flow through the walls and right into the building itself. 'That's what I saw,' said Sheila emphatically.

By now Gaynor was certain too, and she nodded in agreement with Sheila as she gazed up at the old building. Although there had been alterations it was undoubtedly the place in her vision with the decorated walls of the Victorian Gothic revival, the lead divided windows and cobbled forecourt.

Leaving the courtyard they made their way around the main building and into the magnificent gardens. It was here, as they followed the well tended pathways that ran between the symmetrical flower beds and neat rows of evergreen shrubs, that they found what they had seen in the shared vision the previous evening. The low cut privet maze which Mary had seen, and the ornamental bushes cut into the shape of guardsmens' helmets were just as Jean had described them. But most astonishing of all were the two features David had seen. There, high up on the side of the building overlooking the lake, was the carving of an heraldic shield, bearing a device of six daggers exactly matching David's drawing in every detail. Then a bronze statue of embracing lovers protruding from the lake, again just as David described, gave them their final piece of confirmation.

There seemed no reason to doubt that Coombe Abbey was the place in Gaynor's vision. They must now establish the identity of the woman with the Red Stone. Gaynor had not been told her name and could only assume that she had either lived at the Abbey, or, alternatively whoever had lived there in 1865 had been involved in some way with the Order of Meonia.

They left shortly after mid-day and headed for Brinklow Hill, wondering if Mary was right and if it would look like their almost identical drawings. If this was so, there could be little doubt that at the very least the group had shared a unique paranormal experience.

The main road wound still further eastwards towards the quaint country village of Brinklow, then as the road dipped and the hedgerows to either side fell away they were allowed their first unobstructed view.

There on the far horizon, rising high above the village, the huge mound stood out clearly against the blue sky. On the summit were three leafless elms. As their cars entered the village the sign for Brinklow confirmed their arrival. Gaynor had described this strangely rounded hill, but like Jean had seen it without trees. David and Graham had drawn three trees and Martin two. It was as though their visions had given impressions of Coombe Abbey at different times in its past and of how it was today. Only Mary Harrison had previously visited the hill, and that was in her childhood. No-one else present that day had ever before been to Brinklow Hill.

Driving through the village they lost sight of the hill behind the cottages and shops until they reached the parish church at the end of the main street. This fine old building with a castellated tower was set back from the road exactly where they had drawn it at the foot of the hill.

They turned right into the narrow lane that flanked the graveyard and climbed steadily upwards, parking on a grass verge beside a wooden stile and a sign post marked 'Brinklow Castle'.

Brinklow Hill is a huge artificial mound. Some think it was built before the Roman invasion since the Fosse Way meanders round it and then returns to its straight path. Others say it is a Saxon motte and bailey construction, perhaps built on a site of even greater antiquity.

Clambering over the stile and across the silted moat they climbed the hillside. On top the three gnarled elms looked somewhat unnatural as if placed by a giant hand to ward off unwelcome visitors.

From the summit they looked out across the surrounding countryside, a broad plain displaying past and present side by side. The old Roman road passing below from north to south. Grassy banks and ditches stretching away before them, all that remains of what was once a vast fortified area. Tithe barns, farm buildings, church spires, and on the western horizon the twentieth century highrise flats of Coventry. The colourful tapestry of change was breathtaking.

Standing in a group they scanned the horizon, searching for the tower Gaynor had described.

'Have you any idea where it is?' Martin asked her.

Gaynor shook her head.

'If the Stone is hidden there, we'd better find it,' he said.

Gaynor was silent for a moment. 'It's not there anymore,' she said to everyones' surprise. She was unable to say how she knew, but was convinced that though the woman had hidden the Red Stone in the tower when she realised her life was in danger, it was later safely retrieved by Mary Heath once she had succeeded as leader of the Order of Meonia.

The tower was in fact located at a later date about one and half miles to the south-east of the hill. It proved to be the remains of an old priory, the lower section of which now served as a work shed for machinery from the adjoining farm. It surprised no-one to discover that the road the woman would have taken in order to reach the tower from Coombe Abbey went directly past Brinklow Hill.

That day, however, they had run out of time to search further, and Gaynor was adamant that they should still go to Knight's Pool.

* * * *

The cars bounced to a halt on the rocky gravel at the western end of Knight's Pool as a light drizzle began to fall. Just outside the

Worcestershire village of Severn Stoke the lake stands below Knight's Hill, where an eighteenth century domed pavilion was built. Across the countryside meandered the Avon to the east and the Severn to the west.

A narrow, muddy pathway took them to the far end of the lake where in an old stone footbridge the Sword had been concealed. A group of workmen were busy nearby, clearing fallen trees so, not wishing to cause any annoyance or arouse suspicion, Graham asked them if it would be all right to walk around the lake and take some photographs.

'Is it anything to do with the Sword that was found here?' the man asked.

'Yes,' answered Graham, 'how do you know about that?'

'Someone was asking about it this morning.'

'Who?' asked Graham beckoning to the others to hurry over.

The man had little idea. 'Two men and a woman. They walked about for a while, took some photographs and left.' However, when he described the photographer and his yellow Cortina there was no doubting the identity of one of the party: it was Andy Collins.

'They were asking questions about the tower up there,' he said, pointing towards the pavilion on top of Knight's Hill.

Graham enquired about the history of the pavilion, but the man was unable to tell them anything they did not already know. They thanked him and went on their way to the bridge.

'I knew I was right,' said Marion, reminding them all of the strong impression of Andy she had felt earlier.

'I wonder what he was doing here,' mused Martin.

'I told you we should have come earlier,' Gaynor said with a sigh. Her exasperation was quite understandable. If they had taken more notice of her sense of urgency and gone to Knight's Pool that morning they would have arrived at the same time as Andy.

'But why?' asked Martin.

Gaynor shook her head. 'I don't know.'

The group split up and walked around the lake, hoping to find something which might suggest why they had been guided there. Gaynor and Marion stood on the bridge with Terry and Jean, staring out over the cold waters. Knight's Pool seemed almost concealed from the passage of time, tucked away down a small cart track and seldom visited.

By now the air was heavy with drizzle, there were bulrushes and water grasses sprouting through the silt at the waters edge, reaching up to greet the rain. Dead, leafless trees lined the banks, forlorn testaments to the biting winds of winter.

Terry leant over the bridge and peered down at its foundations. It was here that someone long ago had hidden the sword. He wondered if the dark pool still held some other secret that had caused Gaynor to bring them here today. He looked up and caught sight of Sheila Bavington standing about twenty yards from the bridge. She was glancing round nervously as if aware that something was wrong.

'What is it?' called Graham, who had been walking just behind her.

'I don't like this place,' she answered. 'Something's odd about it.'

'In what way?' he asked.

'There's something evil. It's something here now,' she said, shivering. Sheila was experiencing the same awful sense of malevolence she had felt before the appearance of the dark figure the previous evening.

Moments later David's anxious voice called to them from some yards further along the muddy pathway, where he, Martin and Mary were staring up at Knight's Hill. 'Quick come over here.'

They ran along the narrow path to join the other three.

'What is it?' asked Sheila.

'Look,' said David, pointing up at the grassy slopes of the hill. From where they stood they had a clear view through a break in the trees surrounding the lake.

On the brow of the hill was the figure of a man. His black form stood tall and still in clear silhouette against the skyline. But there was something strange about him. They were only about a hundred yards away but they could not make out any of his features. He appeared to be dressed entirely in black, with a long coat and a top hat.

The five of them stood looking up at Knight's Hill, aware that something was wrong. They all felt it, a peculiar chilling sensation, as the motionless figure seemed to stare down at them. It was as if he were waiting for something, standing there just a few feet from the pavilion.

'Look!' cried Martin, pointing to a spot a little lower down the hill. Jean was clambering up the steep hillside toward where the figure stood. She had obviously not seen him, her attention concentrated on her climb. They all shouted to try and warn her, but the wind was against them and she did not hear as she struggled on, oblivious of their calls.

Suddenly she lost her footing and fell to her knees, her fingertips sinking into the mud. Cursing silently she pulled herself up, determined now to get to the top regardless of how wet and dirty she got in the process. For a moment she thought she heard the others calling, but the wind gusted and whistled down the hillside distorting the sound and she went on.

Jean had decided to investigate the pavilion on top of Knight's Hill, in an effort to discover why Andy had been so interested in it. She wondered if he knew something they did not, maybe something involving the history of the building. She considered this might be one reason why they had been led to Knight's Pool that wet and windy March afternoon. She thought she heard the voices calling again but she ignored them as the wind blew more loudly. Another noise now held her attention, it was an uncanny rumbling that grew louder as she neared the top. It felt as if the whole hill was vibrating, resonating in unison with the unearthly sound. It seemed to be coming from somewhere inside the pavilion itself.

* * * *

No-one had noticed the figure slip away while they called to Jean. It should have been impossible for him to have moved without them noticing, but one second he was there and the next he was gone. Jean had disappeared too. They had watched her reach the top of the hill and then go behind the pavilion.

'Come on,' shouted Graham, and he and Martin stumbled along the pathway followed closely by David. As they reached the bridge, however, Jean suddenly re-appeared. She paused for a moment, looking up at the pavilion, then turned and made her way back down the slope.

* * * *

Jean found them in excited conversation as she rejoined the group. For a moment she thought she had missed something, little realising that she had been so close to the black figure on the hill!

'What's all the excitement?' she asked.

David explained. 'But there was no-one up there,' she protested.

Jean was adamant that she would have noticed if anyone had been on the hill. It was suggested that he could have slipped away quickly without her noticing. She insisted that it would have been impossible as she had a clear unobstructed view in all directions. The others wondered if he had gone into the pavilion. But she was certain that if he had she would have seen him, and besides the building was securely padlocked from the outside.

The mystery deepened when Jean explained about the strange rumbling sound that had vibrated the hill. She had in fact spent some time examining the pavilion, searching for a reason to account for the noise. But it had stopped quite abruptly, so unless it had been

a freak wind effect around the pavilion, which she thought
unlikely, there was no explanation. No-one voiced the obvious, but
since the figure had been seen at the same time as Jean experienced
the vibration and noise a connection seemed conceivable.

So who was this man, clearly seen by all five of them, silently
watching from the hill-top? He had appeared only seconds after
Sheila Bavington had felt disquieted and they had all experienced
an uneasy feeling.

As they drove away from Knight's Pool the sky was heavy and
overcast, and the cold waters silent and forbidding. They all had a
strong feeling of some impending danger. Even the comparative
safety of their cars could not wipe away the disturbing image of the
dark clad figure staring down at them from the brow of Knight's
Hill.

This strange episode was a chilling reminder of how an element
of fear could quickly assert itself and that they should never forget
how in the past their investigations had led them into some fearful
situations.

Was their new line of investigation being shadowed by the
sinister looking figure? If so, who, or more disturbingly, **what**, was
he?

## Chapter Three

# An Unknown Legacy

The events of the last two days were extraordinary. By fate or not Andy Collins too had been drawn to Knight's Pool, and they presumed he would be able to throw some light on the mystery.

But this was not to be. Although intrigued by the coincidence of their independent visits to the Pool, Andy was as puzzled as they. He had only gone to take photographs of the lake and the bridge. Neither he nor his companions had any psychic impulse to go there. While at the lake they had not seen or felt anything out of the ordinary, and the only people they saw there had been the workmen.

The mystery remained as puzzling as ever. An attempt to prompt further psychic information at Graham's house proved a disappointment for nothing happened.

Some days later David Bavington suggested that the stone pavilion on Knight's Hill might be worth investigating. The black figure had stood nearby and the strange rumbling noise and vibration felt by Jean had originated from its vicinity. Andy had already explained that he had no special reason for inquiring about the building, but had discovered that it was built for Lord Coventry in the eighteenth century which meant it was there during the Victorian era in which they were interested. With nothing to lose David and Sheila decided to visit the estate and investigate further.

Inquiries the previous year had revealed that the late nineteenth century Earl of Coventry had had no involvement with the Order of Meonia. Lord Coventry's residence at Croome Court near Knight's Pool was until recently the seat of his estate, but today it is owned by the Society for Krishna Consciousness. When they contacted the Society they expressed some interest but were unable to help them further. There appeared to be nothing unusual about the pavilion, just a typical example of eighteenth century architecture.

David and Sheila's research failed to produce anything new, and although they half expected something to happen as they climbed Knight's Hill one sunny afternoon they were disappointed. No strange dark figures appeared, nor were there any mysterious noises, or psychic impressions.

Hopeful that there was still something significant to be discovered Terry took Marion and Gaynor back to the area in late April. But the journey proved fruitless. None of them felt anything, either by the pool, the bridge or on Knight's Hill.

They could only suppose that since no-one had actually seen Knight's Pool in the shared visions of March 20, that the area had no immediate relevance to their search for the Order of Meonia and its' lost secret. Gaynor alone had felt that they should go there, but her impression had come after the experiment had been concluded. Like her mother perhaps Gaynor had psychically 'tuned in' to Andy Collins and 'picked up' that he intended to visit the pool that morning. She freely admitted that this was possible. For the time being then they decided to forget Knight's Pool.

Despite their disappointment they still knew that the evidence of the past three years pointed in a particular direction: the search for the incredible secret held by the Order of Meonia. An extraordinary power source known to the Megalithic peoples three and a half thousand years ago. Now if they were ever to rediscover it they must surely find out what had become of the Order of Meonia during the closing months of 1875. They already knew that the Order had been disbanded in November of that year so the precious secret would not fall into the clutches of the occultist John Laing. A few weeks later they had all fled leaving no trace. For those weeks they had been forced into hiding, and it was during this short time that the secret had been either hidden or passed on to someone else.

Now the question was where or with whom was it hidden. Coombe Abbey sprang immediately to mind. Maybe the answer was there? If the Order had been associated with the Abbey then they must find out all they could about its history or of any connections it had with what they already knew. Graham and Martin resolved to investigate this thoroughly.

After the reformation Coombe Abbey ceased to be an ecclesiastical establishment, reverting instead to being a stately home for many years. Over more recent centuries the owners were the Craven family. Although the name Craven meant nothing to the researchers, they found that the household was involved in certain historical incidents that played an important part in the Meonia mystery. In fact certain events linked by one person, Princess Elizabeth, daughter of James I.

During the search for the Green Stone it was discovered that the

Gunpowder Plotters of 1605 had wished to instate Elizabeth, then still a child, as Queen of England. At the time the plot was hatched Princess Elizabeth was staying at Coombe Abbey. Later in her life she married Frederick V of the Palatinate. It was this marriage in 1613 that the mystical and reformist organisation, the Rosicrucians, proclaimed as the grand alliance, the sign that a new age of intellectual and theological freedom was at hand. There were several reasons for this, but primarily because Elizabeth was seen by many as the prophecied leader of a mysterious new age foretold by astrologers at the time of the Gunpowder Plot. In short, Elizabeth seems to have been the figurehead of the Rosicrucian movement, and it would appear that the leading Rosicrucians of that period were one and the same as the Order of Meonia. But the connection between Elizabeth and Coombe Abbey did not end with the ill-fated Gunpowder Plot. When the Rosicrucian dream collapsed with Elizabeth and Frederick's rash attempt to secure the throne of Bohemia in 1619, after which Elizabeth was exiled, William Craven of Coombe continued to be the chief supporter of her plight and spent many years at her side.

It now seemed possible that Coombe Abbey had been the headquarters of the Order of Meonia, and may have remained so until the time of Mary Heath and the woman in Gaynor's vision.

Another William Craven had owned the estate in 1865, but there was no record of any connection between him and Mary Heath. Considering the shroud of secrecy surrounding the Order this would hardly be surprising even if they had known one another. However they did discover that this William Craven was quite open about his interest in the occult.

Graham and Martin continued to investigate Coombe Abbey for some weeks, until in June Graham left Coventry and moved to London.

* * * *

On the morning of Friday, July 16 Marion was alone in her house in Oakenholt, North Wales. Her husband Fred was away with the Territorial Army and the children were all out. The Meonia mystery was the furthest thing from her mind as she busied herself with the housework.

Suddenly she was startled by a woman's voice calling her name from behind. She turned round in alarm. but there was no-one there. For a moment she was frightened. The voice had seemed so close. She wondered if it could have been someone at the back door. Hurrying through the kitchen she stepped out onto the drive, looking for any sign of a visitor. But the drive was empty. Apart from some young children playing football at the far end of the close the road was deserted. A light breeeze brushed against her face as she checked the back yard and garden shed. They were both empty.

She stood for a short time trying to puzzle it out. There was no doubt about it, she had definitely heard a woman's voice calling her name.

Apprehensively she re-entered the house and went back to the housework. For a moment nothing happened, but seconds later, quite without warning she felt the most peculiar sensation, as if pressure was applied on the back of her head and body. She felt someone, or something, was standing behind her. Fear seized her. She took a deep breath and turned to face whoever it might be. But there was no-one, the room was empty. She heaved a sigh of relief and, with her heart beating rapidly she leant against the door reassured that there was nothing there.

But she was mistaken, for suddenly something brushed past her, almost pushing her back into the doorway.

An invisible presence had entered the house.

* * * *

Terry was at work that lunchtime when his office phone rang. It was Marion, her voice fraught with a sense of excitement.

'Can you get over here tonight?' she asked.

Before Terry had time to answer Marion began to explain what she had experienced.

'Are you absolutely sure there was something there?' he asked.

'Absolutely. It literally pushed me backwards into the doorway.'

'Good grief!' he exclaimed. 'It didn't harm you did it?'

'No, I was frightened at first, but then I felt a sort of warm.....pleasant feeling.'

Marion explained how, although she had seen nothing nor heard the voice again, the distinct feeling that someone was with her had continued for some time. Once the initial shock had passed she became relaxed and calm. Some minutes later she sensed the presence leaving and had a strong impression that she must get the group together as soon as possible.

'Right,' said Terry, 'I'll call the others immediately. Have you got any idea what's actually going on?'

'No, but I do feel it's rather urgent.'

* * * *

At 8.00 p.m. that warm July evening Terry and Alan Beard arrived at the Sunderlands', followed shortly afterwards by Graham with Susan Boyd, a friend from London. Marion explained that she felt another try at getting information by psychic means would probably be successful.

At about 10.30 p.m. with the children safely asleep upstairs, they shifted the sofa and armchairs into a makeshift circle and settled themselves. To help them relax and concentrate Terry switched off the living room light. Now the only light came from the pale orange glow of the streetlamps filtering in through the slats in the closed blinds. But this made it too dark to make a proper record of what anyone might see or hear, so Alan volunteered to stay apart and operate the tape recorder.

Everywhere was quiet except for the faint ticking of the wall clock. Alan sat on a foot-stool in the middle and the others sat back and closed their eyes. He was curious to know if it would work as he sat in silence, looking from one to the other. As the minutes passed and nothing happened he began to fear that the attempt was failing. But then Marion's breathing became more rapid and less relaxed.

'Are you all right?' Alan whispered, leaning closer towards her. But he got no answer.

'Marion?' Again no answer.

Suddenly Alan was aware that something was different, but what was it? Then he realised that the clock on the wall had stopped and the room was in complete silence.

Marion's breathing become more laboured, and in the gloom Alan could just make out her head beginning to move. For some reason he moved back a little, staring at her all the time. Then for a second he froze as from behind a hand grasped his left shoulder. He spun round quickly to find it was Terry.

'For God's sake don't do that,'

Terry apologised. 'Sorry.....is Marion okay?'

'I'm not sure.'

Marion groaned and muttered something indiscernible.

'Marion, are you okay?' Terry whispered urgently, but again she did not answer.

Terry turned to Gaynor.

'Gaynor?'

'Yes.'

'Are you all right?'

'Fine, wide awake.'

'Susan?'

'Okay.'

'Graham?'

Graham did not respond. He just sat motionless in the armchair opposite Marion. In the darkness and quiet of the room a tension developed, an expectant anxiety, an uneasy calm before the storm. Marion let out a deep sigh and relaxed. Terry opened his mouth to speak, but his words were stifled. Then the strangest thing happened, the room began to fill with a hazy blue glow. It grew in intensity, a soft blue light forming as if from the very air itself.

'What the....? What....? Alan was lost for words.

Gaynor grabbed Terry's hand. 'Terry, what is it? What's happening?'

He shook his head quickly and in a hoarse whisper said 'Graham?.... Marion?' but neither moved or made a sound. They were completely silent and still as if in a deep sleep.

Terry gasped as he noticed the source of the light. Unbelievably it was emanating from the bodies of Marion and Graham! And bathed in this strange blue aura their minds were far away in space and time.

* * * *

There was a brilliant whiteness, the dazzling sun shining brightly over the cold winter landscape. Driven snow formed intricate patterns around the scattered boulders littering the deep river valley. On the craggy slopes grew just a few sparse bushes and the occasional leafless tree, rising above the rushing waters cutting their icy path through the steep hills. On opposite banks of the swiftly running river, like the posts of some enormous abandoned gateway, rose two gargantuan pillars of ancient weathered rock thrusting upward into the clear blue sky.

At the base of one of these towering columns was the dark mouth of a cave. Before it stood a girl, clad in weighty furs and a coarse woollen cloak tied at the neck by an ornate silver brooch. Around her shoulders fell a mass of thick red hair.

She stepped from the shelter of the cave and, facing the biting wind that swept down the lonely valley, drew a heavy broad sword from beneath her cloak. She was terribly weary. Fighting a losing battle against exhaustion she raised the weapon above her head and with both hands drove it down into the hard, frozen ground. Taking a short dagger from her belt she knelt before the sword, it's heavy blade shining like burnished gold in the brilliant sunshine. Carefully she began to prize something from the hilt, one of two stones set either side of the cross-guard; one was green, the other red.

Her work completed she stood before the sword, dagger in hand, as the light began to fade.

Just a dim silhouette, the figure remained quite still in the darkness. Then slowly and apprehensively, it edged forward.

'Are you awake?' a man's voice asked. Graham strained his eyes in the gloom as the figure moved still closer. 'Are you awake?' repeated Alan, bending forward, still clasping the microphone in his hand.

* * * *

Later Alan explained to Marion and Graham how they had both fallen into a trance and been surrounded by the strange blue light. But Marion and Graham could only recall drifting off into the vision. They had in fact experienced no sensation connected with the blue aura of light.

'I'm sure I've seen that sword before,' said Marion, 'in a recurring dream. Until now I couldn't make full sense of it. A broad sword, with two stones set into the hilt.'

'What could it mean?' asked Terry.

'I think I know,' said Graham.

The girl in the vision was the Celtic warrior Queen Gwevaraugh and the deep river valley was somewhere of special importance, a site sacred to her ancestors. The scene they had visualised had taken place almost three thousand years ago. The two stones set in the hilt of the sword were in fact the Green Stone they had already discovered, and the Red Stone they had yet to find. As to why the stones were set in the sword Graham did not know.

If the vision of Gwevaraugh and the sword with the two stones was accurate, as previous psychic visions had proven to be, then there was indeed a second stone. A Red Stone that held the key to the ancient power itself!

'I know what the stone was called.' he said, 'The Eye of Fire,' Graham concluded.

'If it's the same Stone that was hidden by the woman from Coombe Abbey,' said Terry, 'where did she get it from?'

'No doubt Gwevaraugh made sure that it could be recovered sometime in the future,' said Marion.

The Order of Meonia must have needed the Red Stone and had somehow been directed to recover it, perhaps in a similar way to which they had found the Green Stone in 1979.

Now at least they understood part of Gaynor's vision of Coombe Abbey and the troubled woman. The secret of the Order of Meonia, the key to the innermost power of the human mind, was the mysterious Red Stone called The Eye of Fire.

They were all quiet for a short time as they considered the implications of this new and dramatic revelation. They had already seen the power of the Green Stone, and now here was an even more powerful artefact, a Stone to unleash the inner forces of the human mind.

Eventually Alan spoke. 'At least we know what we're looking for. The problem now is where to look.'

He was right, of course, for this vision, and those in Coventry, seemed to indicate where the Stone had been hidden in the past, but on both occasions they knew the Stone had been retrieved. What they now need to know was where the Stone was currently hidden.

As far as they knew Mary Heath was the last person to have had it, so presumably she had assured its safety.

'I think I know what happened,' Gaynor said after sitting very quietly for some time. It seemed that she too had had a further vision giving them some of the information they needed and so she explained it to them.

In December 1875 Mary Heath decided that the Order should disband as the risk of the Red Stone falling into the hands of John Laing was far too great. The reason was quite simple, this malevolent occultist had at one time been part of the Order of Meonia. In attempting to seize the leadership from Mary Heath he revealed his true nature and during his attempt very nearly gained the Stone for himself. Mary Heath realised that only by concealing the Stone could its security be guaranteed. The Order therefore disbanded, and its members fled the country to escape Laing and his followers.

Mary Heath spent December 1875 at the home of an old friend, and there made plans to hide the Stone. Before leaving she hid something in the house, something that would lead to the Stone. This was a bell which was to have been collected by someone to whom she sent instructions. Unfortunately, however, this person died before having a chance to retrieve it.

'Are you certain of all this?' asked Terry as Gaynor paused.

'Yes I am quite sure,' she said.

'And do you know where this bell is?' queried Marion.

'I know the name of the house.' Gaynor continued. 'It's called Ranton Abbey.'

Terry knew of the abbey already. It is a large old house in rural Staffordshire, that like Coombe had long ago ceased to be a monastic building. It had once served as a hunting lodge for the Earl of Lichfield, but today is a remote and derelict ruin, having been gutted by fire during the second world war.

'Ranton Abbey's pretty big,' said Terry. 'There must be a thousand places to hide something.'

'Well, I'm sorry but that's all I got.' answered Gaynor.

After some discussion they agreed to visit Ranton Abbey as soon as possible. However, Gaynor seemed concerned.

'What's wrong?' Graham asked her.

She paused for a moment before saying anything. 'This might sound pretty unbelievable but I feel I must say it.'

'Go on,' said Terry.

'The Red Stone holds great power. A power that Mary Heath used to protect the bell.' Gaynor paused before continuing, concern still showing on her face. 'She created a guardian.'

'A guardian?' asked Terry. 'What do you mean?'

Gaynor explained how Mary Heath had used the Red Stone to create a powerful thought-form, and its sole purpose was to protect the bell from falling into the wrong hands. It could remain inactive for many years until someone entered the house in search of the bell. Quite how this activated the Guardian, let alone how it could exist at all, Gaynor had no idea.

Mary had programmed the Guardian to stop anyone who came in search of the bell. Anyone, that is, except the person she intended to find it. But unfortunately this person had died prematurely. So even though the group were not enemies the Guardian would respond to them as if they were.

'So you see we must be very careful,' concluded Gaynor.

'It's not that I don't believe you, but how do you know all this?' asked Susan.

'I just do.' Gaynor replied, 'I know I'm right.'

'Perhaps we shouldn't go,' said Alan standing up. 'We might be getting involved with something which is none of our concern.'

'If it were none of our concern then surely we wouldn't have been told about it.' Marion said.

Alan reluctantly agreed.

'So how does it work?' asked Graham. 'What can the Guardian do to us?'

Gaynor explained that the Guardian was able to use the primeval fears deep within the mind. It could draw out these basic fears, the latent nightmares of the psyche, and make them a terrifying reality turned against anyone who attempted to remove the bell.

Everyone fell silent again. Certainly the possibility of being confronted by their deepest nightmares was a very disturbing prospect.

'Perhaps if we take the Green Stone we'll be all right,' suggested Marion.

Gaynor shook her head. 'I'm afraid it wouldn't do us any good,' she said.

'The Green Stone could overcome any abuse of the power, but Mary Heath used it for protection which is a different thing altogether. I'm afraid it wouldn't help.'

'I don't think we need to worry much,' said Graham hopefully, 'it seems that the Guardian can only create illusions. As long as we remember that.....'

'You're wrong,' interupted Gaynor. 'It can do much more than that.'

# Chapter Four
# The Living Dead

Saturday, July 24, had come warm and dry, and in the air was that occasional midsummer feeling that all was well with the world. Overhead the cloudless blue sky was peaceful and reassuring, as if the day could last forever.

The two cars wound their way along the narrow country lanes that meander through the tiny hamlets just north of the county town of Stafford. As they drew nearer the derelict Abbey at Ranton, they exchanged few words as the fearful prospect of their task became clearer with each passing mile. Unless they could find the bell they would be unable to discover the ultimate secret. They had to find the bell, it was the only key to discovering the Eye of Fire.

A narrow dirt track took them away from the lanes, through open parkland dotted with chestnut trees and occasional grazing deer. The cars bounced on the uneven surface, jolting their occupants already frail nerves. In one car there was Terry, his wife Pat, Alan, Gaynor and Marion, and in the other Graham, Martin and Susan. Animals in the fields turned their heads at the sound of the approaching vehicles, blissfully unaware of what might befall the troubled occupants.

Martin jumped out and held open the gate as the cars passed through. Securing it behind him he could not help but feel he was sealing their last line of escape and perhaps with it their fate.

The lush foliage surrounding the ruins buzzed with the sounds of summer. A thick mass of trees, bushes and evergreen shrubs obscured the buildings as they approached, a colourful barrier of blossom and greenery alive with insects and tiny creatures. Passing through a leafy archway they came at last into the inner sanctum of the ruins.

Their first sight of the Abbey was spellbinding. There was a powerful grey stone tower rising high above the trees as if oblivious of the crumbling red brick lodge below. Standing proud in its sentinel-like position, this is all that remains of the original Abbey.

Once called Essairs Abbey, it was founded by Robert Fitz-Noel in the reign of Henry II. Although occupied by monks of the Augustinian Order as early as 1150, the edifice itself was added in the 15th century and the four windows, in a line one above the other, indicated that it was once used as a dwelling. As they gazed up at the tower in the lengthening shadows of early evening, Terry was the first to voice the unspoken concern they all felt.

'How on earth are we going to find a hiding place in there?' he said. 'It'll be like looking for a needle in a haystack.'

'We'll find it,' said Gaynor. 'We've **got** to find it.' She fell silent for a moment then spoke again. 'It's not in here,' she said. 'It's over there.' She was pointing towards the ruined hunting lodge. Less than fifty yards away, built around 1820 but now in ruins, the large hunting lodge stands within the shadow of the tower. The building of the lodge meant that the Abbey church, the remaining low walls and small portion of the cloisters had never been excavated. Perhaps then the bell had remained undisturbed.

The dilapidated lodge appeared quiet, almost resigned to its irreversible decay. Ivy was cascading down the outer walls in a tumble of greenery so that only its lower windows could still be discerned. The roof had long since fallen away into the heavy shadows of the gloomy interior. Outside the lodge appeared rustic and inviting, a rarely visited and little known place. But within the high broken walls, patched unevenly with creeping vines, there lay an unknown sense of menace. Submerged within the shadows of the enclosing walls large brown rats scurried from room to room, along empty passageways and deep into rancid holes. Somewhere inside, concealed amid the turgid air heavy with contempt and bitterness, there lurked a creation of darkness. An incalculable terror to be unleashed upon those who dared to seek the legacy within its charge. Now the day of its purpose had arrived, but for those about to enter the place nothing could have mentally armed them for what they were about to face.

As the others wandered around the outer walls, Marion stood examining the facade, looking at the patchwork of tumbling ivy and twisted creepers before her. She felt as if the walls had eyes, narrow slits of green that were angered by her presence; silently waiting, ever watchful and brooding. The whole place gave off a disquieting aura, almost a malevolent awareness of their intrusion.

Leaning back against the trunk of a tall oak standing between the tower and the lodge, Pat momentarily forgot their predicament, her thoughts taken by the soft evening sunshine. But suddenly a woman's voice broke through her reverie, calling her name from somewhere inside the lodge.

'Quick Terry,' she called, and started picking her way over the coarse rubble towards the archway that led into the crumbling building. She paused at the entrance, held back by a sudden sense of danger. Terry came up behind her.

'Someone called me,' she said. 'It was a woman's voice.'

'It must have been one of the others.'

'I don't think so,' said Pat. 'Something is wrong.'

Together they stepped forward into the building.

\* \* \* \*

Something awoke

\* \* \* \*

A surreal vision lay before them. To their left a long corridor, old and thick with decades of rubble, and to their right the floor falling away into a high, roofless chamber, melancholy and still except for the faint but persistent sounds of the slowly crumbling masonry. Over the years the plaster had gradually fallen away in patches revealing the wooden laths beneath. Heavy black charred timbers lay across the room at awkward angles. Small trees, knotted and twisted, had somehow forced their way upward through the debris, only to be strangled by gaunt, half dead creepers, smothering everything as if with hairy arms.

What had once been the upper floors, long ago broken away by rot and decay, were now no more than a few pitted timbers thrusting out from the walls into empty space. This bizarre chamber was an unnatural place, an irksome combination of nature and human creation, thrown awkwardly together in a parody of order.

'My God! exclaimed Terry, 'I've never seen anything like it.'

'Quiet,' said Pat, urging him to silence as she searched for the source of the voice she had heard. She was sure it had come from where they now stood, at the end of the corridor beneath the archwayed entrance. But there was no-one to be seen. The passageway felt heavy and sick with years of waste, rank and musty, somehow defiant of the beautiful summer's evening which barely intruded on the chill gloom of the interior.

'I don't like this place,' Terry said slowly, 'I think we'd better find the others.' And with that they turned and hurried from the building, glad to be back in the fresh clean air. The oppressive atmosphere of the lodge had rendered them almost oblivious to the fact that they had found no-one to account for the voice calling Pat's name.

Marion made her way round the outside of the dilapidated building, peering through the windows long ago having lost their glass. At last she found an unobscured doorway from where a long corridor led to a high room. Two timbers had fallen at right angles forming a twisted cross about half way down its length.

Momentarily she caught a glimpse of Terry and Pat standing at the far end, partly visible in what was obviously the archway entrance. She was about to call out when they turned and disappeared from view. Marion was surprised by the degree of uncertainty she now felt. But it was there, an uneasy clawing at her mind, a presence of fear and contempt for her and her friends. A shiver tingled down her spine, as she tried to steel herself to enter.

Marion froze as a woman's voice called her name from the far end of the passageway. The voice did not sound like Pat's. But **someone** had definitely called her.

Without a second thought she crossed the threshold and started down the passageway. Almost at once the walls seemed to close in about her, looming overhead, beating down their dank oppression. The air was harsh and bitter, stale and heavy in her nostrils as if it had been breathed many times over. She was quite alone. Her steps quickened, almost to a run as she sensed the watchfulness all around her. Arriving suddenly at the room she halted abruptly, only just in time to see that the floor fell away in front of her. She was standing on the edge of a ten foot drop onto jagged moss covered stones. Though the woman's voice had called from here, there was no-one in sight.

'Marion?' said a voice, and her heart missed a beat as she span round.

'Oh, thank God it's you,' she said, breathing a sigh of relief as Pat and Terry joined her. 'So it was you who shouted me, what did you want?'

However, it quickly became clear that Pat had not called Marion nor vice versa. The voice remained a complete mystery.

'I don't know who it was,' said Terry, 'but I intend to find out.'

He set off along the corridor until half way down a noise suddenly alerted him. It sounded like a faint exhalation of air, old and troubled. Glancing round he saw nothing but the empty passageway. He strode on, picking his way carefully over the two fallen cross beams and on down the claustrophobic gully with the walls rising some forty feet on either side. His nerves became increasingly alert with every step, more conscious that he was drawing nearer and nearer to something horrible. The walls seemed to close in over him; his heart quickened.

Three doorways led off to the right, spaced evenly along the fifty foot length of the passageway. As he reached the first, he stopped and looked back. Marion and Pat were nowhere to be seen. It was now his turn to feel completely isolated. Terry let out a sigh as if to steady his increasingly jumpy nerves and stepped through the doorway to find a small room. The floor of what might have once been a study was now a mass of tangled bellbine, bricks and plaster. A window opening faced him, half covered with hanging ivy. Something about the room made him decide not to enter. He continued along the corridor. The air was sickly with the aftermath of the day's heat, stale and lifeless. Terry was almost at the second doorway when in the gloom he caught a swift movement out of the corner of his eye. Something had moved in the corridor behind him. He quickly turned to face it, just in time to catch sight of something disappearing into the room he had just passed. He thought it might be Pat or Marion. Fear that it was not almost held him back, but he edged forward, perspiration breaking out on his forehead as he prepared for a confrontation.

Then with a rush of determination he entered the room. It lay empty and silent, there was no-one to be seen. His heart pounded as he scanned the interior. There was only one way in, whatever had entered the room was still there. Terry began to feel cold and his whole body began to feel heavy and drowsy. Then something moved over to his left. He turned, but at that moment an enormous shadow seemed to lurch from the wall and sweep over him, tearing at his mind and body. He shook uncontrollably as the malevolence engulfed him. A sweet nausea punched at the hollow of his stomach and bent him double. He felt that at any second he would pass out. Through the sickly haze the realisation dawned. Something had lured him into the room. He must escape, but could not think how, there seemed nothing he could do.

Suddenly it was gone just as mysteriously as it had come. What sunlight there was threw welcome light onto his strained face as he slithered awkwardly to the floor, his back against the wall.

Terry wiped the sweat from his hands, and raising himself clumsily to his feet clutched the wall for support and staggered from the room back into the corridor. After what seemed to him like hours but could only have been seconds later, he fell into Pat's arms.

* * * *

'Whatever it was I'm afraid that's what we've got to beat if we're ever going to get this bell,' said Marion. 'It's not going to be easy.' She smiled positively, but her encouragement seemed wilted by Terry's frightful experience.

Meanwhile Graham, Susan and Gaynor had been scouring the outside of the lodge in search of any likely hiding place. A narrow opening at ground level next to the archway led them down a pile of rubble into the complete darkness of the cellars. Years of undisturbed cobwebs draped the flaking whitewashed walls, hanging like net curtains from the masonry. Cold and dank, the air hung very still while their narrow torch beam swung to and fro as they huddled into the first chamber.

'What better place to hide something,' suggested Susan.

'I don't know,' Gaynor mused. 'I don't think we should stay down here for too long.'

After some minutes of moving from room to room they came upon a three foot wide hole in the floor.

'Careful,' said Graham, aiming the light at the opening.

'A well!' exclaimed Susan, 'this could be it.' Although only a yard wide the well was over ten foot deep, the torch beam reflecting off the clear water below.

'If it's in there we've had it,' said Graham, 'there's no way we could reach it without risk of serious injury.' Gaynor suddenly interrupted. 'It's not down there.' She took the torch from Graham's hand and made for the exit tunnel. 'We must get out of there,' she said. 'Something's wrong.'

* * * *

Outside Terry was recovering in the waning light as the sun sank lower in the evening sky. By now everyone was becoming increasingly anxious. Time was pressing and as yet they had found absolutely nothing. Terry had suffered a ghastly experience leaving him drained and almost too frightened to stay, and now Graham, Susan and Gaynor had disappeared.

The unease was temporarily lifted with the welcome appearance of the gamekeeper, who had seen the cars and wandered up the drive to check who they were. They told him that they were interested in local history and he responded helpfully. He said that the hunting lodge had belonged to Lord Lichfield in the last century and during the Second World war it was used to billet a squadron of Dutch airmen who, the gamekeeper claimed, were so disturbed by the oppressive atmosphere of the place that they set it on fire so they would be moved elsewhere. What remains today is little more than the crumbling shell left by the fire. Partly explaining their interest in the lodge, Marion told the gamekeeper of their search for a hidden bell. He said that the Abbey and estate now belonged to the Wedgewood pottery group and, as far as he was concerned, since the building was no longer of any value they were welcome to look around. However, he advised them to be very careful as the building was not at all safe.

* * * *

In the cellars Graham, Susan and Gaynor stood rooted to the spot in petrified silence. Somewhere ahead heavy footfalls padded slowly and persistently towards them. The sound of laboured breathing and a sickly stench preceded whatever it was that approached. The breathing penetrated and echoed loudly from the darkness around the sharp bend in the corridor. In seconds it would round the corner and be upon them.

'Run, for Christ's sake!' screamed Graham, pushing Gaynor and Susan ahead and running blindly along the dark tunnel behind them. Glancing back he tried desperately to focus the torch on their pursuer. But the beam was beginning to die. His eyes met only a more intense blackness than already cloaked the tunnel. It was such a complete blackness, seething within itself, shapeless but at the same time having substance. He choked back a cry of fear and ran faster to catch up with the girls. A vile odour flooded his nostrils like the sweet smell of death and decay. In horror he recalled what Gaynor had said. The Guardian of the bell could simulate the primeval fears of the human mind: the realms of darkness and the unknown. The abomination that approached was to each of them their most dreaded fear.

It drew ever closer, gaining ground with each passing second. Gaynor screamed in horror as she stumbled along the tunnel. She was crying with tears of fear and mental torture streaming down her face. Taking one last anguished step they reached the opening and the stack of rubble, which was their only escape route to the outside world.

Graham crouched at the bottom of the rubble stack waiting as the two girls tried to haul themselves out through the narrow opening. - **For God's sake hurry**. - The footsteps - heavy dragging feet. The breathing, slow, laboured and reedy - the stench - overpowering, putrid, vile, - they came ever nearer. - **Please hurry**. Gaynor had caught her foot in the brickwork and was frantically struggling to free herself.

The abomination in the darkness was now only twenty feet away. Graham's heart was racing, and cold sweat stung his eyes. Again he turned the torch to the passage behind him, but the bulb was now just a dim glow illuminating no more than four or five feet ahead. It seemed as if something in the tunnel was actually draining power from the torch. Graham knew that whatever it was he would not see it until it was upon him, in fact it might be the last thing he ever saw. His stomach began to convulse and he began to heave, retching at the sickly sweet stench.

'For God's sake hurry!' he cried, panic welling up inside him.

Then Gaynor was free and Susan was pulling herself out. With the dreadful presence no more than ten feet away Graham scrambled up the rubble pile, squeezed through the opening and out into the sunshine.

As if it had never really existed the shadow slipped back into the black cellars, leaving them shaking with terror as they collapsed on the bricks outside the lodge.

\* \* \* \*

Everyone except Martin stood outside the Abbey Lodge.

'This is absolutely ridiculous,' Graham choked, 'we can't go on like this. Someone's going to get hurt. That's it, we're going, sod the bell, sod it all.'

'I'm afraid we've got no choice,' Gaynor answered, biting back her tears. We've already gone too far, we can't stop now.'

The daylight was fading as the sun dropped ever lower.

It was setting as a great crimson disc in a beautiful evening sky, the light ebbing slowly away. If the Guardian fed on the primitive fear of darkness it was becoming more powerful by the moment. Their time was agonisingly short.

'Where's Martin?' Marion asked. They all looked quickly around, but he was nowhere to be seen.

\* \* \* \*

Inside the large room at the end of the corridor Martin clambered over the fallen timbers, making towards a separate area of partly exposed cellar. The room had an unreal quality, the lonely shell of a once inhabited place. Shards of masonry had peeled and fallen to the floor, littering the room with rocks and dust. Gnarled trees lay in strange formations across the ground and against the flaking lichen covered walls. The heaviness of the air seemed almost to hold back his progress, as if the very room itself hated his presence. Precariously balanced pieces of stone seemed to stare threateningly down from high upon the once ornate walls, bearing down on the solitary figure, alone in a strange jungle of desolation and decay.

Scanning the cellar opening by torchlight, then looking back and taking in the size of the room behind him, he was hard pressed to assure himself that there might still be some chance of success. Many of the walls had indeed collapsed, but a good proportion remained. As he began to despair of them ever finding the bell he was suddenly aware that he was not alone.

A harsh laboured breathing rasped horribly from somewhere in the room. Martin froze. It sounded like a great beast awakened and stirring to life. He looked around but could see nothing. He heard it again, this time louder and from somewhere above. He stepped back, letting out a sharp gasp of alarm as the unearthly sound seemed to sweep down upon him.

Quite abruptly it ceased. Martin found himself against the wall, his arms outstretched, his heart pounding; involuntarily paralysed with fear as if staring in petrified silence at a giant cobra, poised and ready to strike at the slightest movement.

Then came the sound of a slow and deliberate exhalation of air only feet in front of his face. But there was nothing to be seen. The air though was full of some presence, a sweet sickly smell like rotting meat forced its way into his lungs and nausea welled up inside him.

Suddenly all was silent again, but he knew it was still there, he could feel it. Something quite terrible and unseen, an invisible predator stalking its prey. In his mind he could almost see the abomination that faced him, its razor sharp teeth, its vile salivating tongue, then his head began to spin,

The air became icy cold as the disembodied breathing began again, slowly, but then more rapid, he felt it was about to pounce.

Martin was trapped. The corridor, his only way of escape, lay thirty feet away across the twisted and mangled derrangement that had become the room. In a last desperate effort of sheer will he tore himself from the wall and ran for his life. A black hollowness filled his mind, casting away the last vestiges of reason as he stumbled blindly on, his hands beating wildly at the air above his head to fend off his unseen attacker. Each second became a lifetime as he tumbled and fell across the room. Every step a nightmare of confusion. At last he fell against the pile of bricks below the doorway and clawed at it painfully, searching for a handhold. Breathless, he choked back the heaving in his throat, scrambled over the rubble and launched himself into the air, his hands just managed to grab the jagged stonework of the corridor floor above. He hauled himself up with the last of his strength and collapsed exhausted on the ground. Had the others not arrived at that moment, it is difficult to imagine what might have happened.

* * * *

They all stood huddled together under the spreading branches of the large oak tree in the courtyard, carefully considering their situation.

'I'm convinced the Guardian is stronger in the dark,' said Marion after hearing all the details. 'It makes sense.'

She explained her theory. So far, their bizzare encounters at Ranton Abbey had all occurred in dark places: Terry had been in the small, dimly-lit chamber, Gaynor, Susan and Graham in the pitch black with only the failing torchlight to guide them, and Martin in the darkness of the partially exposed section of the cellars.

It seemed that the Guardian was either badly affected by daylight or, more probably, judging by what Gaynor had originally told them, the primeval fear of darkness, etched so deep within the human mind, somehow gave it the greater power it needed.

'If you're right we'd better stay out in the sunlight,' said Graham, 'although that'll stop us from searching a large part of the ruins.'

Marion appeared deep in thought. Then she said, 'There may be a way. I think I might be able to stop it if I can somehow convince it that we are meant to be here.'

To everyone's surprise Marion announced that she intended to stand in the ruins and summon the Guardian.

'You must be joking!' Martin exclaimed.

'I don't think you appreciate the power of this thing,' said Terry. But Marion was not listening. She had made up her mind and set off towards the ruins, closely followed by Gaynor and Susan.

'We'll wait out here.' shouted Terry, as the three women disappeared through the archway.

* * * *

They stood at the end of the corridor looking out over the derelict room. Susan and Gaynor fixed their eyes on Marion as she spoke aloud.

'Guardian, we are meant to be here, please understand.'

It happened immediately. Marion had hoped that the Guardian would hear. She had not expected it to return, not in the light. But she was wrong.

The disembodied breathing came harsh and loud from somewhere high up on the opposite wall. It was a troubled rasping sound that sent a judder of fear through her body. Thrown by the sudden turn of events Marion had to make a choice, either she turned and fled or she confronted the invisible being. The two girls stepped back as Marion almost unconsciously made the decision to fight it out. As the awful sound grew louder she began to visualise a force of pure light to envelop the thing that faced her. The breathing quickened as if in preparation for some terrible event. She focussed the full power of her will.

The horrible noise ceased and Marion relaxed. Letting out a deep sigh of relief she turned to Susan and Gaynor and was about to speak when a great hissing sound shattered the silence around them. Then Marion knew that she could not win.

The power that had created the thought-form Guardian was greater than any of them could comprehend. The breathing returned, louder and more virulent than before, coming closer and closer until it was upon them. A wave of uncontrollable terror swept over Marion, becoming more and more violent, until in a last moment of utter defiance Marion screamed. The terrible noise cut dead and she collapsed on the floor.

* * * *

Having been carried from the ruins Marion sat with her back against the oak tree, pale and shaking. Her head throbbed violently, her whole body was drained of energy.

'That's it,' said Pat, 'we're leaving now.'

No-one disagreed until Marion suddenly interrupted.

'We can't,' she said, her voice breathless and faltering. 'We can't leave now. If we do we'll never find the bell.'

'Damn the bell.' Pat said. 'This is far too dangerous.'

Marion shook her head. 'You don't understand,' she said. As they stood about her in uneasy silence Marion explained her feelings. She thought that the Guardian had exhausted much of its power during its confrontation with her.

Although they must be extremely careful, she felt the force that moved against them would now be more limited in its influence, but only for a short time. It would soon recover as the daylight finally faded.

'We have until sundown,' she said. With the sunset the power of the Guardian would return. What they had so far encountered would be nothing in comparison to what they could expect once night began to fall.

'Why don't we leave it for today and come back in the morning,' suggested Pat.

'Because the Guardian has been awakened,' said Marion gravely. 'It will only become stronger. If anyone ever comes here again looking for the bell, even during daylight, they wouldn't stand a chance.'

They were not certain she was right, but it may be conceivable that she had gained some insight into the nature of the macabre entity that stalked the ruins of Ranton Abbey. She implored them to trust her.

'We've got to make a decision,' said Gaynor, who had been sitting quietly with an arm around her mother. 'If we really do want to find the Eye of Fire, we must find the bell. We either do that now or forget the whole thing.'

They all looked at one another, each weighing their desire to discover the truth, the secret of Meonia, against their sense of self preservation.

'Are you sure it'll be safe until sunset?' Terry asked Marion.

'Not completely,' she said, 'but once dusk comes....'

'Look, we can't waste time,' interrupted Martin. 'Does anyone know what time the sun goes down?'

Alan checked his diary.

'We've got half an hour. I suggest we give it till then.'

Everyone agreed. They quickly decided that Marion ought to stay outside. Gaynor and Alan would stay with her. After some argument Terry persuaded Pat to remain also.

At 8.40 p.m., the sun now dangerously low in the sky, Terry, Graham, Martin and Susan re-entered the gloomy interior of the derelict hunting lodge.

The four of them split up and hurriedly went from room to room in the slim hope of discovering clues that might lead to the bell. They had no further psychic messages to go on and no-one that evening had received any form of inspiration, apart from Gaynor saying the bell was in the lodge. There were no visible indications, no hint of a concealed hiding place. They were lost in a labyrinth of debris, floundering without direction.

Martin and Graham met up in the long corridor and entered into frantic debate. Where would Mary Heath, or anyone for that matter, hide something so that it might be recovered at a later date? The choices were endless; the cellars, underneath the floor, the walls, they were all equally likely.

Suddenly a rumbling noise echoed overhead, and with it a huge section of masonry plummeted forward off the highest point of the wall. Martin saw it just in time. The heavy section thundered down towards Graham. In a split second Martin leaped forward and thrust him violently backwards, the pair of them came crashing to the floor only inches from where the great chunk of rubble splintered into a thousand pieces a second later.

The brick-fall was large enough to have killed both of them.

'For God's sake!' gasped Graham.

'Let's get the hell out of here,' shouted Martin.

They raced down the corridor, almost knocking over Susan and Terry who appeared from one of the side rooms.

'Run!' yelled Martin. And they did. Under the archway and out of the lodge.

* * * *

Gaynor and Alan were searching around the exterior of the building. But their efforts were useless. Every place they tried produced only bits of wood or discarded tin cans.

As they reached the far side of the derelict lodge they heard a terrible crash followed by Graham and Martin's frantic shouting. Quickly they hurried to the doorway that led into the corridor from where the noise had come. But there was no-one to be seen. Graham and Martin had already fled.

As Gaynor and Alan exchanged puzzled glances, each wondering what might have happened, a peculiar sensation suddenly overcame them. It was as if the air had become charged with electricity. A weird prickling numbness spread over the exposed parts of their skin.

Alan saw it first. 'Gaynor, look!' His voice betrayed a mixture of amazement and horror.

In the thin layer of sand covering the step in front of them something was forming. As if traced by an invisible finger a pattern was taking shape before their very eyes! A five pointed star. They recognised it immediately, the inverted pentagram. The occult sign of death and destruction.

* * * *

They all gathered by the doorway, staring down at the diabolical symbol drawn in the dust on the step. They seemed to have been given a final warning, with only minutes before darkness would begin to fall.

There were such frightening things happening. Events that were not only terrifying but which questioned their conception of reality.

'There's nothing we can do,' said Alan. 'Even if we risk going back in there for the few minutes left before sunset we don't know where to look.'

'Alan's right,' said Martin. 'We'd be risking our necks for nothing. We've had no help and we haven't a clue to go on'

'Oh yes we have.' said Gaynor springing up from the large stone on which she had been sitting.

'Something **was** helping us.'

Everyone looked at her, puzzled.

'Don't you see? Once we entered the lodge we awoke the Guardian and she was stopped from helping us further'

'She?' said Graham, 'what are you talking about?'

'Yes, of course.' Marion looked skywards in a gesture of self recrimination. 'The voice I heard, the woman's voice.'

'She called our names,' interrupted Pat, reminding them that she too had heard this mysterious voice.

'Who was she?' Graham asked.

'No time for that now,' said Terry, 'go on Gaynor. What do you think it means?'

'Perhaps she was trying to lead us to the bell,' she said, 'call us to the right spot. But once we went inside the Guardian prevented her.'

In a few excited moments they reasoned it out.

The voice of a woman had called both Pat and Marion by name, summoned them into the ruins. Each was sure the voice had come from somewhere near the end of the corridor, just inside the archway, where the floor fell away into the largest room. It had been here that Marion had stood and confronted the Guardian.

'Then it must be there,' said Gaynor. And without another word she jumped over the step and raced into the Lodge.

* * * *

They had no choice but to follow her. The seven of them crossed the forbidden threshold and reluctantly made their way down the long dark passageway to join Gaynor at the far end.

'If it is here,' motioned Terry, 'it must be sealed up behind the plaster. But the question is, where?'

'There's only one way to find out,' said Alan, and he hurried off to his car. A few moments later he returned, carrying a hammer and crowbar from his tool kit.

'Stand back.' shouted Terry. He swung the hammer at the wall to the right of the doorway, and with a dull thud a large section of plasterwork fell away and crashed down to the room below.

And then the nightmare began.

* * * *

'Oh my God.' Martin's voice was a hollow, dry whisper, but the terror it conveyed froze them all.

'Look!'

In the dank gloom at the other end of the corridor something was moving just where they had entered only a few minutes before, a featureless shadow shifting like a dark spectre across the narrow passageway. Then there was another - and a third.

It was impossible. Dark obnoxious figures were rising from the cellars. Marion screamed in horror as an awful stench hit them, that same sweet sickly odour of decaying flesh drifting in waves from the dark humanoid forms that now stood grotesque and menacing, silhouetted in the light of the doorway. Transient phantoms with no real substance, or were they solid material obscenities, whatever the true nature of these vile apparitions none of them dared think.

Even as they stared transfixed at the pandemonic scene, from behind came the sound of the Guardian, The Lord of the living hell that now surrounded them. The harsh reedy breathing resounded through the huge chamber, so dreadful and hideous it chilled their very souls. Even the lodge itself seemed to recoil, subjugated by the assault of manifest anger.

Alan dropped his crowbar and fled through the archway as Marion grabbed her daughter's arm and turned to follow.

'No!' shouted Gaynor. 'We still have time.' She pulled away from her mother, picked up a heavy brick and thrust it into Graham's hand.

'Use this.' she commanded him. 'Try the other side.'

He stared at her and then at Terry who had stopped hammering after the first blow.

'Terry. Carry on,' implored Gaynor, 'Please!'

The two men stood looking past her toward the motionless forms some fifty feet away.

'Please!' shouted Gaynor.

They obeyed her imperative voice.

Working frantically, dust and debris splintering about them, Terry and Graham hammered away at the walls on either side of the doorway. Piece by piece the lath and plaster fell away to reveal the dark-red brickwork that lay beneath.

The dark forms began to move. They shuffled along the corridor towards them like reanimated corpses, or strange vampiric creatures risen by the power of vengeance from the grave. The obnoxious reek filled the air more potently than before. Marion retched and clutched her stomach as Susan picked up a heavy length of charred timber and stood defiantly beneath the archway.

'For God's sake,' she shouted. 'Hurry.'

Still the breathing grew louder, snorting down from somewhere above. Then it swooped down at them from the large chamber, a violent hiss rising to an intense wailing scream. Then there was a blinding flash of crackling blue light arcing across the doorway. It struck Graham head on, going right through his body with a massive jarring shock and throwing him backwards against the opposite wall. He was motionless for a few seconds, staring ahead with unseeing eyes, then he fell to the floor, unconscious.

Dark featureless creatures, shadows brought to life, their arms hanging by their sides, their feet dragging in mindless unison. The atmosphere still permeated by their horrendous stench, overpowering and sick. Now the hellish shapes were within five yards of where they were.

Terry's mind was reeling. Repeatedly he hammered at the wall, frenziedly tearing away the loosened plaster with his free hand, panic welling up within him. He was concentrating with all his might on not running, trying to hold on as long as he could. He was only partly aware of what was happening about him ... he dare not look ... dare not even think ... he must keep going ... keep going ... He heard the noisy breathing again, the high pitched hiss and then another flash jolted the wall. He heard Marion scream. Plaster dust and pieces of brickwork fell about him as out of the corner of his eye he saw someone slump to the ground. It was Marion. He turned. Pat was standing over her.

'Pat, get out,' he shouted frantically. Behind her he saw half a dozen looming forms, now only feet away.

He took one last desperate blow at the wall and a large section of plaster fell to the floor.

Then he froze. Before him, on a narrow enclave hidden beneath the lath and plaster, lay a small bronze bell, green with age and no more than five inches high. He just stared, unable to move for what seemed like an eternity. Then he stirred into action and grabbed it with both hands.

'I've got it.' Terry's voice was quiet and unbelieving.

Gaynor, Susan and Pat just stared at him. Then he shouted. 'Get out ... Run!'

Like the strobing images of a magic lantern, a series of still but fleeting scenes, the next few moments were to burn deep into Terry's memory, never to be forgotten. There was Susan, Pat, Martin and Gaynor staring at Graham lying still and lifeless at the foot of the wall. Then Marion crawling on all fours, trying to fight her way to her feet. And worst of all, the absolute limit of human terror. The Living Dead. Sweet corpses, arms outstretched, fingers waving insanely, coming to eat his body.

The hideous breathing reverberated deafeningly in their ears. The whole lodge seemed to rock and shudder from its rage as splinters of masonry began to tumble from the high walls and black shadows seethed in the darkness. Marion forced herself to stand and stumbled through the arch, Pat followed while Gaynor and Susan dragged Graham's unconscious body across the rubble.

Terry stood in the corridor for a last, split second as the others staggered out of the ruins. The dark shapes came together and took on a bizarre ameboid form. Then they became lost in the dense cloud of acrid dust that rained down upon them. It seemed as if the whole place was about to collapse, and with a great cry that froze his blood the presence of the Guardian exploded about him. Terry turned and fled.

Pushing Graham into the back of Terry's car they tore away from the scene. Reaching the gate Martin leapt out and flung it open while the cars raced through. Slamming it behind them he turned and glanced westward.

The crimson orb that had been the evening sun dipped silently below the far horizon.

## Chapter Five
# The Secret

Terry was shattered. He sat in the passenger seat as Alan drove them away from the Abbey at speed. He clutched the bell in both hands, almost in a state of shock.

His mind flickered from one thought to another, remembering the hammering, the loathsome breathing behind him, then the plaster crumbling away, and there in a small recess, the bell.

'What have we done,' said Alan.

Terry forced a smile and shrugged. 'Let's get home and talk about it then.' All he wanted was to put as much distance as possible between them and the godforsaken Abbey.

As they sped away from Ranton only Pat and Alan were in a fit state to drive, although even they were affected by the feeling of nausea experienced by the others. The journey back to Terry's cottage at Saverley Green was tense and apprehensive. They had certainly found the bell, but no-one had any idea what to do next.

They drew up outside the house. It was a dark, clear evening. The lights of the cottage shone out to greet them, a welcoming confirmation that they were safe, at least for the moment. During the drive they had more or less recovered, that is everyone but Marion. In confronting the Guardian to gain extra time she had been totally drained. Her face was still very pale and she was badly shaken, to such an extent that Pat suggested her seeing a doctor. But Marion insisted she would be all right after a cup of tea and a good night's sleep.

As she rested the group discussed their predicament. They were unsure what to do next. As far as Pat was concerned though enough was enough. She was not prepared to go through anything like that again. She was adamant that she wanted nothing more to do with it, and protested Terry should do the same.

'But what about the Red Stone?' he objected.

'For all I care,' she replied firmly, 'it can stay hidden forever.'

'But we're safe now. We've got the bell.'

The others agreed with Terry, but Marion insisted that it was now becoming much too dangerous for her to allow Gaynor to accompany them on any further investigations. Naturally Gaynor protested she would be quite all right, but Marion was not prepared to take any more risks. It was one thing to receive psychic visions and race round the country to verify them, but quite another to face such real danger.

It was almost midnight before Terry and Pat's visitors departed. Alan gave Martin a lift home, and Graham and Susan took Marion and Gaynor back to Wales, staying overnight with them.

* * * *

Green with the verdigris of a hundred years the bronze bell stood just five inches high. On top was a small loop through which it must once have been suspended.

Why had Mary Heath gone to such lengths to protect it from falling into enemy hands? And how was it to lead them to the Red Stone, The Eye of Fire?

What was it's secret?

* * * *

Terry and Alan travelled to the Sunderland's house the following afternoon, where Graham and Susan had already spent many hours pondering over the bell. Earlier in the day Fred Sunderland, after hearing an account of the frightening episode at Ranton, suggested that they should clean it. But they were reluctant to do so. The general consensus was to take the bell to local historians at the earliest opportunity, where they could confirm its age and might even identify its original use, which might be their only lead to finding the Red Stone. Although Fred wholeheartedly agreed, he was quick to remind them of the Knight's Pool Sword. It had been the inscription along the blade of the Sword that had led them to the Green Stone. There might very well be a similar inscription on the bell, and if so finding it quickly could again be of the essence. There was no choice. If it was inscribed with a message they had to know: immediately.

So for some hours the bell had been standing in a deep bowl of their only available cleaning agent, brown sauce.

Fred lifted the bell from the solution and wiped it clean. The sauce had proved effective, most of the verdigris had been removed. It was not quite clean, but enough to clearly see the entire surface.

They examined it carefully, inspecting the dull metal for signs of any inscription.

But although they had successfully cleaned the bell the result was disappointing. There was no inscription or design of any kind, either inside or out. Nothing whatsover, no writing or message.

'Now what?' asked Graham, when they had carefully examined their precious find.

No-one answered. Their disappointment was understandable because they had all pinned their hopes on the bell providing a clue to discovering the Eye of Fire, but now they were baffled.

'The solution to the mystery must be the bell itself,' suggested Alan. They stared at him blankly.

'Well,' he continued, 'Why should the means of finding the Stone be a bell at all? Why not something else?'

Alan had a point. They should consider why Mary Heath chose to hide a **bell**, for if it was simply to contain a message then she could have used a carefully boxed letter. This, however, had obviously been too dangerous. Presumably she could not risk such a clear direction falling into the hands of John Laing. So the only logical solution was that the bell itself must have meant something to the person it had been hidden for.

'Perhaps the Stone is hidden where the bell came from,' said Alan. If they could manage to find where the bell had once hung, then they might come closer to understanding its significance.

'What sort of bell is it do you think? Terry asked.

'I'd say it's a servant's bell,' replied Marion. 'The kind that used to hang in the scullery of a large house.'

If Marion was right then where would they begin to look. There must be thousands of old houses large enough to have employed domestic help at that time. Their chances of finding the right one seemed slim. Graham suggested they consult an expert to help them.

'A bell expert?' Alan asked incredulously, 'Is there such a thing?'

'An antique dealer maybe.'

'I honestly don't think we can do that,' Terry intervened.

After a somewhat heated discussion they eventually agreed with him. Until they knew more they could not afford to tell anyone else about the bell. It might even prove dangerous to do so.

It was ironical that they were unable to find out more without expert advice, but they could not chance seeking that advice until they found out more.

There appeared only one way to take things further, and that was another attempt to gain information by psychic means. Marion asked to be excluded this time. She simply did not feel up to it, she still hadn't recovered from her frightful ordeal the previous day at Ranton. Fully understanding Marion's trepidation they decided to make the attempt somewhere else.

Since Pat would not have the bell in her house Terry suggested Graham and Susan take it with them to see if they could discover anything new.

\* \* \* \*

They were unaware how they were getting their psychic information or in what way they managed to tune their minds to events in the past. It was possible it was happening by clairvoyance or maybe some other way, perhaps some form of intelligence was helping and guiding them. Maybe it was a combination of both. Wherever the information originated it was not to prove helpful with their search in finding an answer to the bell mystery. Although others had received psychic messages they centred primarily on Marion and Gaynor. Consequently, all attempts to gain the necessary psychic information without them failed to produce any worthwhile results. With no more clairvoyant help they were left to unravel the enigma by logical deduction.

They must try and find from where the bell originally came. They could only assume that this was one of the places seen by Gaynor and the others during the visions in mid March. Gaynor had been certain of one thing in particular, and that was that the Red Stone was **not** at Knight's Pool. They were therefore left with the possibility of it coming from Coombe Abbey. This seemed quite likely since it was a stately home where a large domestic staff would have been in service. If there was something unusual about the servant's bells at Coombe, possibly a unique design that matched the one they had, they would undoubtedly have something to go on.

Martin and Graham decided to investigate whether Mary Heath could have concealed the Stone at Coombe Abbey.

The grounds were almost deserted that particular Tuesday afternoon as they left the car-park and crossed the footbridge into the cobbled forecourt.

'That's interesting,' said Martin staring up at the information plaque on the yard wall. 'Coombe Abbey was founded in the same year as Ranton, 1150.'

'Do you think that could be relevant?'

Martin shook his head. 'Probably not, the monks here were Cistercian. The Ranton monks were Augustinian.'

They left the courtyard and made their way through the broad archway and on to the inhabited part of the old residence, the original stables and outbuildings that had been converted into houses for the permanent staff now responsible for the upkeep of the Abbey. By good fortune they found someone to help them almost at once, it was the head warden, Robin Moore.

Robin Moore had, for the past few years, been preparing a detailed history of Coombe Abbey and was, therefore, a mine of valuable information.

They briefly told him the unusual circumstances in which they had first heard of the old place and that they were currently researching its long and eventful history. To back up what, to Robin Moore, must have seemed an incredible story they showed him copies of the drawings made on the evening of 20 March.

'What about the cellars?' asked Martin, holding out David Bavington's sketch.

'They're here all right,' he answered, 'below the cloisters.'

Martin and Graham exchanged a quick glance. If they were the same then perhaps it was here that the bell had hung. Maybe at long last they were on the right path.

The warden was so intrigued by their story that he offered to show them the cellars there and then.

'They were built between 1863 and 1865 by William Craven,' he explained. 'But quite what went on down there no-one seems to know for sure.'

He led them back across the courtyard to the Neo-Gothic wing that overlooked the moat. Then he stopped before an old lancet doorway and pointed to two strange carvings over the entrance.

'Goodness knows why old Craven had them put there,' he said, unlocking the door. Carved into the stonework were a coiled serpent and a goat's head, both ancient occult symbols.

Once the light had been switched on they found themselves in a winding corridor, its dirty whitewashed walls peeling with age. Musty air wafted into their faces as they followed him, along narrow passageways, across the creaking floorboards of bare, dusty rooms and finally through an oak panelled doorway opening on to the grey stone steps leading down into the cellars.

Could this be the place where the troubled woman in Gaynor's vision had come to retrieve the Red Stone? The air became cold and damp as they descended, their footsteps resounding across the sandstone walls while the sound of dripping water echoed somewhere below.

The chamber that met their eyes was like an ancient storage room or medieval dungeon, about forty feet square with high arches springing from square stone pillars to support the roof some ten feet above their heads.

Daylight streamed in through the wooden portcullis partially obscuring the broad archway through which the moat flowed. Dark muddy water filled half the expanse of the cellar floor. It was an underground wharf, a sheltering place for small rowing boats.

Having business to attend to the warden left them to look around on their own.

'This is the place all right,' said Martin moving into a corner. 'If you stand about here David's drawing shows it exactly as it is.'

'And the portcullis,' added Graham. 'It's the one Sheila pointed out from the bridge.' He positioned himself at the waters edge and leant over to see outside.

'Yes, this is it.'

'It's uncanny.' Martin took out his camera and began taking some photographs. 'Gaynor told us that what she had seen happened in 1865, it's the same year this place was built.'

'It's a damn pity that she didn't actually see what the woman did once she got down here,' said Graham.

'She must have got the Red Stone from somewhere.'

'Yes, but where?'

Martin shrugged. 'Goodness knows, but how can that help?'

Graham explained his theory. If the woman in Gaynor's vision had left the Stone here at one time then maybe Mary Heath had also made use of the same hiding place.

'Behind one of these stones perhaps?'

They scanned the walls, half hoping for some form of psychic guidance or intuition to help them. But nothing happened and it seemed they must solve this one for themselves.

If anything was hidden in the cellar there was certainly no obvious indication as to where abouts. They could do nothing more. Even if a hiding place did exist, armed only with an old servant's bell and an incredible story they would find it very difficult to convince the relevant authorities to allow a potentially destructive search of the place.

Anyway such a request would no doubt take weeks, if not months, to process. Time they did not have. Without more to act on they could knock down half the building before finding anything.

'We can't even be sure the woman retrieved the Stone from here at all,' said Martin sitting down on the stone steps. 'Going by what Gaynor said she could have had it with her all the time.'

Graham had to agree. If the vision was accurate, and so far it seemed it was, then the woman might have entered the cellar for some other reason.

Martin looked around, looking concerned.

'What's wrong?'

'Craven may have been her enemy,' he said. 'The goat's head over the doorway. Do you reckon this place could have been used for black magic?'

'I don't know, but it could mean exactly the opposite. Medieval stone masons used to carve grotesque demons in the belief that they would ward off evil.'

Fascinating as their visit to the cellar had been they were still no nearer discovering the secret of the Ranton bell. It seemed unlikely that it had hung down there, and if they could not prove that it came from anywhere else in the building then they might very well be wasting their time at Coombe Abbey altogether.

When Robin Moore returned, they asked him about the servant's bells in the main Abbey buildings. He said that no doubt there would have been such bells, but they were not there now and hadn't been for many years. As far as he knew there would have been nothing unusual about them.

As they drove away from Coombe Abbey they discussed the situation. The vaulted cellar was almost certainly the one David had drawn and presumably the place Gaynor had seen in her vision of the victorian woman. But they did not know what to do next.

Their only chance seemed to be Brinklow Hill. Since four of them had been led to draw it, it must hold some significance. Perhaps the Stone was buried somewhere near this ancient landmark.

Looking out over the landscape that sunny afternoon they were confronted by the same dilemma they found at Coombe Abbey. If the Stone was buried on the hill it would be almost impossible to find. To dig indiscriminately would be pointless and foolhardy, not to mention illegal since the hill is a protected monument.

A light breeze brushed across the grassy hill as Martin leant against one of the three twisted elms. Graham paced back and forth across the summit, thinking hard. He paused for a moment and surveyed the landscape. Coventry's famous three spires rose high over the distant horizon, vague silhouettes in the afternoon haze. A constant traffic flow tailed along the Fosse Way far below the hill.

He kicked his feet and turned to Martin. 'Well now what?'

'The church perhaps,' Martin ventured. 'It appeared in the drawings.'

'The church it is,' said Graham, turning and picking a careful path down the steep hillside.

They crossed the ditch and stile and went down the lane to the main road. The Fosse runs straight through Brinklow, being the main street around which the village grew up. Quaint thatched cottages stand side by side with modern semi-detached houses, one of those rare places where the new has not tainted the old.

A hundred yards from the lane they came to the church, set back on land rising up to meet the lower ramparts of Brinklow Hill.

The quiet old church rose high over the surrounding houses, for half a millenium the central feature of village life. Once inside, the church's sparse and silent interior greeted them with heavy cold air musty with the smell of slight decay. However although they discovered one or two interesting architectural features they found nothing relevant to their search.

Emerging into the sunlight they decided to investigate the churchyard. Set between the houses and overlooking the village high street the place had a strange tranquility all of its own. The newer graves in front of the church were well tended and the surrounding grass neatly cut. But on the steadily rising slope behind the church were older graves, overgrown and forgotten, dating back to the eighteenth century. Scrambling through the thick under-growth they examined the gravestones, straining to read the faded inscriptions.

It was just possible they might recognise one of the names. But they were disappointed, for apart from scratches and nettle stings they got nothing from their exploration of the old burial ground.

'We don't seem to be getting anywhere,' said Graham.

Martin turned and looked towards the hill. For a split second it was almost as if he knew something, but then it was gone. He stood in silence and stared at Brinklow Hill.

'What's wrong?' said Graham. Martin shook his head.

'I don't know,' he said, 'but I'm sure the answer's staring us in the face.'

* * * *

Alan was concerned. It was less than a week since he had last seen Marion, but in that short time her whole appearance had altered dramatically. Instead of her usual fresh bright self she looked haggard and withdrawn. Her tired eyes were ringed with deep black shadows.

She explained that since the bell episode she had found no difficulty in sleeping, in fact she had slept surprisingly well, but despite this she was completely rundown. Even the smallest physical effort left her absolutely exhausted. Everything she did drained her of energy.

'The doctor thinks it's vitamin deficiency,' she told Alan, 'he's given me some tablets.'

Although she assured him that she would be all right in a day or so Alan was not so sure. He could not help feeling that there was some connection between her state of health and the events that had overtaken them at Ranton Abbey. She had been fine before that time but immediately following the visit the peculiar, fatiguing malady had begun. At first it appeared that Marion was simply tired after their ordeal. But it had continued, and it was disturbing to see her anything other than bright and cheery. He hoped the doctor's judgement was right and that her strange condition was nothing more serious.

Alan and Marion sat in the Sunderland family's living room discussing Alan's new theory about the bell.

'I think I've an idea where the Stone might be hidden,' he said. 'I'm still certain that the visions we've had should be able to help us.'

'Possibly,' said Marion, 'but Graham and Martin have been checking them and as yet they've drawn a blank.'

'I know, but we've been forgetting the other vision. The one where the blue light shone from you and Graham.'

'Go on,' prompted Marion.

'I think Mary Heath may have taken the Stone to where Gwevaraugh hid it.'

Marion thought carefully before agreeing. She leant over and took a notepad from the sideboard in which she had recorded the details of the vision. She handed the pad to Alan, and he scanned the notes, taking in the geographical details. A cave, a cave in a deep river valley and two huge pillars of rock. Such an outstanding landmark would be easily recognisable if they saw it, but first they had to find it.

'Have you got any idea where it is?' asked Alan.

Marion shook her head. 'I'm sorry, it could be anywhere in the world. I do wish we had something more to go on.'

'Maybe we have,' replied Alan. He took out a pen, and turning to a fresh page in the pad began to make notes.

'Number One, Gwevaraugh lived in England, the centre of England to be precise. So I reckon it's a safe bet that this place is somewhere in or near the Midlands.'

Marion nodded. 'That's still a pretty large area.'

Alan continued to write. 'Number two. A deep river valley or gorge ... and the description of the cave suggests a limestone area.'

'How many limestone areas are there?' enquired Marion.

He replied with a confident smile. 'I don't know yet, but it's a start.

Alan was pleased that Marion agreed with his theory. He felt sure that this line of thought would ultimately prove rewarding. . Before he left that night he told Marion he would try and find out as much as possible about any limestone areas in the Midlands. He would ask his work colleagues and consult all available literature.

Alan was excited as he drove home in the early hours of morning. He was sure he was right, and if he was, and such a place did exist, he reasoned that it would almost certainly look the same today. Unless of course it had been artificially altered, though somewhere in the back of his mind he knew it would be the same. They **would** find the place, he was sure.

* * * *

When Graham picked up his phone Terry's voice was loud and excited.

'We've found the place in your vision,' he announced.

Terry explained Alan's theory concerning the cave in which Gwevaraugh had stood. He had narrowed down his options and found illustrated books covering the areas involved.

'Alan's here at the moment,' continued Terry, 'I've seen the photograph of where he thinks the place is. The valley looks right and so do the two pillars of rock, one either side of a river.'

'Where is it?' asked Graham eagerly.

'It's a place called Ilam Rock along the Dove Valley in Derbyshire. We're sure it's right but you'll have to see for yourself.'

'What about the cave?'

'We can't say for sure, but there are plenty of caves in the area.'

Like Marion, Graham agreed with Alan's theory that Mary Heath could well have taken the Red Stone to where Gwevaraugh had hidden it. It was logical to use such an ancient and sacred location.

'I'll be over this weekend.'

* * * *

At 6.30 p.m. Graham was in his London flat watching television when a peculiar sensation suddenly overcame him, a feeling that something was dreadfully wrong. He tried to dismiss it and concentrate on the programme, but the impression remained and intensified.

Whether he wandered across the living room by chance or as a response to some kind of unconscious impulse he would never know, but pulling back the net curtains he looked out onto the open space surrounded on three sides by seven storey flats. Thirty feet below him on the quadrangle, steam was rising from the concrete. It was hot after a day's unbroken sunshine and a recent shower was evaporating into the warm summer evening. A group of children on bicycles rode playfully around the square, laughing and shouting. People walked this way and that, criss-crossing the busy precinct. Some, commuters from the city, eager to be home, others, boisterous youths, setting out early for a good night on the town. The whole area buzzed with life, the hustle and bustle of a metropolitan city.

But as he looked down on the scene Graham became suddenly aware of the reason for his concern. The hairs on the back of his neck seemed to stand on end as he caught sight of a man standing in one corner of the precinct. Beside a shopfront was someone completely out of place in that typical suburban scene, someone a century beyond his time.

Graham shuddered as an ice cold chill ran through his body. He took a deep breath and leant forward through the window, his hands gripping tightly on the ledge. There was no doubt about it, this was the same dark figure he and his friends had seen on the brow of Knight's Hill, clad in a black frock coat and top hat. There he stood right in the middle of London! The motionless figure seemed to be staring up at him intently, but the distance between them prevented Graham from seeing his face clearly other than thick whiskers or a beard. He did however feel the same chill malevolence, the gnawing sense of evil.

For a moment he just stared. Then he ran, breaking away from the window and racing from the flat. If the man was human he would catch him. If not ... But even as he ran he knew full well that the figure was the sinister watcher they had seen at the pool. He took the steps three at a time, almost knocking over a young couple in his rush to get downstairs. Pounding across the concrete he burst out through the double glass doors into the sunshine. But the figure had disappeared.

He strode to the shopfront and quickly scanned the quadrangle. It just wasn't humanly possible for the man to have vanished that quickly. He asked two boys outside the shop, but they had seen nothing unusual.

He had not really expected to be able to catch the mysterious watcher. As before he had melted into thin air, so with a last glance around the precinct Graham returned to the flat and poured himself a stiff drink.

This second sighting of the strange figure perplexed him even more than the first. The man had returned, made himself visible in a busy housing area, and this concerned Graham.

He did not know who or what the figure was, but most disturbing of all he did not know what it wanted.

## Chapter Six
# The Cave

When Graham travelled to the Shotton's Staffordshire home that Saturday he was more optimistic than he had been for some time. He remained concerned about the appearance of the mysterious watcher, but Alan's discovery of the cave's location gave him new hope. Something told him they were drawing nearer their answer.

Terry ushered him into the living room of the cottage, talking excitedly about the fresh turn of events, and as they entered Alan looked up from the table, which was covered with books, maps and diagrams.

'We're nearly there,' he began, 'Marion's already confirmed that it's the place she saw in the vision.' He pushed an open book across the table and pointed at two full-page colour plates.

'Ilam Rock and the Dove Holes in Dovedale, South Derbyshire. Dovedale is a notable Midland beauty spot.'

Graham sat down and examined the pictures. In the first stood two huge pillars of grey rock rising high over the banks of a river. Beneath the rocks a wooden footbridge crossed the water, connecting the outcrops on either side.

'That's the place all right,' said Graham.

'The cave below is called Pickering Cave but it looks too small to be the one you described,' said Terry.

Graham pointed to the plate on the opposite page which showed two large shallow caves cut into a steep limestone hillside. 'The smaller of the two on the left, that's the cave I saw, I'm absolutely sure.'

'Right,' said Terry, taking the book and placing it on the table, 'we'll go tomorrow.'

* * * *

The next morning was bright and fresh as they left the house. They all wondered if Alan had found the right place. Graham was almost sure, but only a visit to the actual spot could confirm it for certain.

Leaving the outskirts of Stoke-on-Trent and travelling on through the lush green fields of rural Staffordshire they made their way into the foothills of the Derbyshire Peak District. The road wound its way across the rolling moorland, over wide open fields divided by grey stone walls, passing small buildings and occasional cottages. In time they came upon great stone tors, thrusting out from sparse grassy tufts and shallow topsoil where wayside boulders lay, deposited long ago by the retreating glaciers of the ice age. Here youthful streams, fed by the peat stained waters seeping out through the dark loam, trickled between the rocks. Upon this barren and desolate upland stand isolated stone circles, earthen mounds and solitary monoliths, lasting testaments to the megalithic race.

In the time of these ancient peoples the land was not so bleak and unwelcoming as now. The climate was more temperate, better suited to the demands of a pastoral way of life. For hundreds of years they lived undisturbed, a stable and organised community living in harmony with nature. Such was the extent of this stability, that the culture spread and developed over most of the British Isles, and only after the climate became colder and less hospitable did the society change. Some turned to violence and warfare as a new and expedient way of life. The more peaceful migrated south and east to escape the ravages of the emerging barbarians. Today this area might seem little more than a desolate and sparsely inhabited moorland, but once it housed an ordered community, an ancient race dwelling in the rich dales and warm open fields.

The car descended the steep winding road at the northern extremity of the valley.

'This is it,' said Alan, slamming the door and stretching his arms. They were parked on a small gravelled area next to the river in the tiny hamlet of Milldale, a cluster of stone houses nestled at the head of the valley. The smiling faces of the daytrippers and hikers reminded them that Dovedale is not only a site of ancient mystery, but also a popular and picturesque tourist attraction.

They crossed the stone footbridge into the green dale. The spectacular gorge stretched away into the far distance, a sheer narrow valley gouged into the soft limestone by running water, wind and rain. In parts, where the harder rock has better resisted erosion, huge crags and pinnacles project out from the steep slopes. Some are lichen covered, but for the most part they stand bare, grey and massive, silent guardians to the tranquility of the gorge. Here and there are caverns and archways, and strangely contorted rocks giving the appearance of grotesque animals.

It is also a valley of lush vegetation, marking the county boundary between Staffordshire and Derbyshire. To the east the heavily forested Derbyshire side, and to the west Staffordshire, in parts even more wooded. But at Milldale the abrupt and almost sheer slopes are dotted only with the occasional bush or tree. Here scree tumbles down almost to the waters edge, the busy river slicing its way through the precipitous valley.

'Good grief,' gasped Terry. 'What a fantastic place.'

Alan led the way, followed by Graham, Terry and Pat. As they walked along they took in the breathtaking scenery, the fresh rushing waters, the awe inspiring slopes and the timeless calm of the gorge.

About a mile further on, the pathway dipped into the trees, forming a tunnel of greenery, rich with the smell of summer. Seconds later they emerged to stand before the Dove Holes, two gaping caverns in the limestone some twenty feet above the rushing water below. Nearest was the smaller cave, a shallow hemisphere some fifteen feet wide and high. A little further on the second was deeper, some fifty to sixty feet across and thirty feet high.

Graham stood back, surveying the impressive natural rock formations.

'Well?' said Alan.

'That's the one,' answered Graham, pointing to the smaller cave.

Alan marvelled at the scene, and considered the possibility of finding the answer to their mystery here. He wondered if indeed a great Celtic warrior queen and her people had made this place sacred in a far off time, and whether Gwevaraugh had stood before this cave, as Graham and Marion had witnessed in their vision.

* * * *

Terry returned from his investigation of the larger cave.

'Well if the Stone is hidden here goodness knows where it is'.

'So what do we do next?' Pat said.

'Obviously the bell is the key,' said Alan, his voice echoing from the smaller cave. They followed him in and looked out over the river winding timelessly around a bare exposed rock that thrust out into the waters. On the other bank the Shepherd's Abbey Rocks, two adjacent limestone blocks partially covered by lichen and gorse, above which the steep slope rose high into the misty grey haze at the summit.

'I'm sure we're overlooking something,' said Alan, 'something quite obvious.'

'What?' Terry asked.

'I'm not quite … I've got it,' he suddenly exclaimed, '**ring** the bell!'

Everyone looked confused. 'We've rung it plenty of times,' said Terry.

'I know, but perhaps it has to be rung in the right place,' replied Alan.

Terry hesitated for a second, then held up the bell and struck it with his fountain pen. It rang out in a high shrill note, a clear sound rising and falling, echoing across the mouth of the cave. Suddenly the whole place seemed to shudder and vibrate, as if the very rock itself were resonating in unison with the bell, reverberating in answer to it's call.

'My God,' shouted Alan, calling out to make himself heard, and clasping his hands over his ears. Graham stared in disbelief, and Pat was unable to speak. Terry covered one ear, holding the bell at arm's length with his other hand.

For some seconds the strange vibration resounded across the rocks, a chiming wall of sound washing over them like a great angry wave. And then it faded, subsiding away, slipping back into the cold stone. Slowly the afternoon stillness returned and the cave was calm once more.

Alan lowered his hands and looked about cautiously, half expecting something to happen. Terry carefully placed the bell on the ground. The cave was still, empty and silent,

'I don't think we'd better try that again,' he said falteringly, 'Goodness knows what might happen.'

'Goodness knows what did happen,' interrupted Pat, still shaking.

'I don't know,' said Alan.

After some discussion they decided it would be best to leave. Although Alan and Graham were eager to hear the bell rung again, Pat and Terry thought it more prudent to contact Marion and Gaynor before proceeding further. After such an unusual event they were not prepared to take unnecessary risks. Perhaps the bell had become somehow charged, perhaps it had acquired some unknown power. There was no way of telling. Both these and more troubling possibilities crossed their minds, settling their decision to leave and return at a later date with reinforcements.

Before leaving they resolved to check out Ilam Rock, its mighty pillars towered high over the River Dove, two great limestone pinnacles grey and bare in the afternoon sunshine. Looking at these, underlined for them that it was undoubtedly the place. Crossing the rather unstable wooden footbridge to the base of the second pillar they found Pickering Cave, a small opening littered with debris and full of stinking mud. This short detour confirmed that the vision had linked together the Dove Holes and Ilam Rock.

Leaving the pillars they made their way back along the gorge, past the caves and scree slopes and finally into Milldale. For most people Dovedale Gorge remains a picturesque beauty spot, a gem of English scenery, but that afternoon it had assumed a new and mysterious countenance. Now there was an air of uncertainty, a sense of impending revelation and discovery.

* * * *

Later that day the four sat in the comfort of Marion's home in Oakenholt near Flint. The children played outside, unaware of the importance of the meeting going on inside. Only Gaynor sat quietly listening as Alan and Terry recounted the day's events. Marion was excited and surprised at what she heard.

'It was incredible,' concluded Alan, 'absolutely incredible.'

'Of course,' said Marion, 'the tone of the bell must be a specific and somehow special note.'

'But how does that help?' asked Pat.

Marion thought for a moment. 'I think it's a signal of some sort,' she suggested carefully, 'a code or calling sign if you like.'

'Open Sesame?' said Graham, half seriously.

Marion nodded and smiled. 'Yes, something like that, but less to open a doorway and more to act as a password to call on someone or something.' She explained her feelings. Mary Heath had created a powerful thought-form guardian at Ranton Abbey and this had acted to protect against anyone but the right person rediscovering the bell. How this was possible they could not begin to understand, but faced with the very real and frightening events at Ranton Abbey they could not deny its existence. Whatever it was, there was no question that it had physically and psychically attacked them.

If Mary Heath had somehow created such a tremendous force to act as guardian, it was reasonable to assume that she could also create a guide. A guide which would lead them to the Stone when triggered by the tone of the bell.

'You mean ring the bell and the guide will appear?' Graham asked.

'Precisely,' said Marion.

'But we rang the bell, and no-one came,' said Alan.

'I think you got half of it,' Marion went on. 'It's the right place but the wrong time. I think it has to be done at a certain time on a certain date.'

Alan seemed puzzled.

'Remember what happened at Ranton. The Guardian was most powerful at night.'

Marion was right, of course, the Guardian had become ever more powerful and vicious as darkness grew nearer. They shuddered to think what might have happened had they not found the bell, and managed to leave the Abbey before sunset.

'If the Guardian was stronger after dark then perhaps the guide is too,' said Marion. 'You obviously experienced the stirrings of the guide, but it couldn't manifest itself visibly because it was too light.'

Terry smiled weakly as he considered the implications of what Marion was saying. Had darkness fallen while they were at Ranton the Guardian itself could have become physical and attacked them. He dare not think what abominable form it might have assumed.

'Well I for one don't fancy going up that gorge in the pitch black,' said Alan nervously. 'Apart from breaking every bone in our bodies, who knows what we might be letting ourselves in for.'

'Well, this guide is obviously benevolent,' said Marion.

'I know that,' Alan answered, 'but what if there's something trying to stop us like there was before?'

'Nothing suggests there is,' said Graham.

'Nothing suggests there isn't,' said Alan. 'And what about this 'watcher' figure? I don't like the sound of him.'

In their exuberance at having located the cave and rock pillars they had temporarily forgotten the dark figure whose identity and purpose remained unknown.

'We can't be too careful,' said Alan, 'I am not happy about struggling along a pitch black gorge at the dead of night being shadowed by some mysterious and probably horrible thing.'

'Me neither,' said Pat.

But Marion was sure it would be all right, adding that they must make the trip the following weekend. Sunday 1st August was Lugnasadh, an ancient Celtic fire festival. If they were there as the day began, at midnight, she was certain it would work. They left that night with a mixture of emotions. Fear that the dark watcher was perhaps shadowing their every move. Concern at what next Friday might bring, and a feeling that something very significant was about to occur. In just a weeks time they would know.

# Chapter Seven
# The Summoning

Alan, Mike, Graham, Martin, Jean and Susan assembled at Terry's cottage that evening and were joined shortly after by Joe Larosa, a friend of Terry's who knew something of the events so far and had asked to be included. Around 10.30 p.m. the group left the house and ventured into the night, a convoy of cars twisting and turning along the narrow lanes of rural Staffordshire before climbing high onto the deserted moorlands of the Derbyshire Peak district. The headlamp beams snaked around each bend, taking them ever closer to God knows what.

For the most part they all remained silent throughout the journey, their thoughts dwelling on what the night would bring.

After descending the winding track leading down to the head of the gorge, they arrived at last in Milldale and parked on the gravel at the river's edge. The sleeping village was dark and peaceful, unaware of its night-time visitors, the foreboding silence broken only by the babbling waters and the irregular calling of a distant owl. They spoke in hushed whispers, endeavouring to stay quiet for fear of waking the inhabitants, as it would be difficult to explain their activities to concerned villagers, worse still, they might not make the caves in time.

Alan elected to stay behind and wait with the cars. It might be a long wait, possibly all night, but they all agreed that someone needed to stay in case suspicion was aroused by their presence.

The sky was clear and speckled with cold white stars, the night air still and dry. A cool breeze swept along the valley as they crossed the footbridge and entered the gorge. The very atmosphere around them seemed charged with emotion. No-one knew quite what to expect nor what unseen dangers lay ahead. Primeval fear tugged at their already fraught nerves as they wondered if the dark watcher was stalking them from behind or maybe somewhere ahead in the night. They tried hard to dispel such thoughts, but as the gorge shrouded them in a cloak of darkness it was hard to dismiss their growing anxiety.

Faces set and intent they continued along the muddy pathway, seven huddled figures following the guiding light of Terry's torch. The valley was sinister and unnerving at night, a strange inhospitable place appearing almost aware of its uninvited guests. Macabre shadows moved in the torch beam, branches swayed in the breeze and animals scurried away from the approaching light. A heavy curtain of blackness lay before them, an impenetrable night had fallen on the gorge.

Everyone suddenly stopped, and Graham tumbled into Susan and muttered apology. For a moment all their stomachs tightened, uncertain why they had suddenly halted. But it was just Terry, pausing momentarily to consult the map. 'This is it,' he called, letting them know they had arrived.

It was nearly midnight as, in the depths of the craggy gorge, the group clambered up the rocks towards the mouth of the cave. Terry stood at the entrance apprehensively shining his torch into the stony recesses in the cold interior. The others protested below as they were left in darkness, robbed of the guiding light of their only torch. Terry apologised and turned his back on the gaping cavern. Down below, the rushing waters of the icy river cascaded over stones and boulders creating a strange noise that echoed eerily around the deep expanse behind him, adding to the peculiar atmosphere of the rocky chamber.

They set about making a small fire to stave off the clawing cold. The dry sticks soon kindled and a welcome light filled the cave, a solitary island of warmth and comfort in the dark isolation of the valley. It was like a crackling beacon burning in the heart of the ancient rocks, a shield against danger and the cold black night outside. They stood close about it, drawing new strength and reassurance from the leaping flames.

After some discussion it was agreed that Terry should ring the bell since it was he who found it. It was now two minutes to midnight.

Terry stepped forward from the cave, stood silently for a few moments then struck the side of the bell. It rang out loud and clear, it's high tone merging with the sound of the river before it died away on the soft wind. They exchanged nervous glances as the flames danced and flickered.

Nothing. The only sounds were the constant but muffled rush of the water and the hissing and crackling from the hot embers of the fire.

Terry turned and shrugged. 'What now?'

'Try saying something.' suggested Martin.

Terry thought for a moment before turning and striking the bell for a second time. 'I have come for the Stone,' he said. The bell rang out, but again there was nothing, only an echo drifting out onto the wind.

'Perhaps the Stone's still on the Sword as Marion and Graham saw in the vision,' said Mike. 'Try asking for the Sword.'

'I have come for the Sword,' cried Terry, ringing the bell a third time.

The valley was unmoved, timeless and deserted offering no response. It would not yet yield it's ancient secret.

Placing the bell in his bag Terry rejoined them round the fire.

'What about waiting for dawn,' said Terry. 'First light, perhaps that's the right time.'

After some discussion they agreed to his suggestion. They would await the dawn and try again, and if that was unsuccessful they would make a final attempt at sunrise. There were three hours to wait. It was to be a long cold night of speculation on what, if anything, would happen at first light. As the hours passed slowly by they were glad of the fire, its wholesome flames staving off the chill breeze blowing up from the icy river below.

Martin curled up on the rocks at the back of the cave and snatched a few hours sleep. Terry paced up and down, unable to rest or dispel his concern that they might have missed their chance.

Joe stood at the mouth of the cave, peering into the inky blackness shrouding the valley, and listened to the river slowly eroding its incessant path through the gorge. When Terry had told him of the strange events that had so affected his life he had found them difficult to accept. Now here he was, cold and tired in the cheerless gloom of an isolated cave in the middle of nowhere. He was beginning to wonder what he had got himself into. But there was nothing he could do now. He had to stay, wait it out until morning and see what happened.

The hours passed and dawn approached. Slowly the night began to fade as the blackness gave way to a valley of vague silhouettes. Shadowy crags and pinnacles of stone set amongst the trees, the far horizon still merging with the night sky. A white carpet of mist hung above the river as a bird stirred and became the first of the chorus to reaffirm its territory for the coming day.

A strange impending atmosphere filled the valley as dawn came. In silent accord they looked expectantly towards Terry as he took the bell from his bag.

No-one spoke as he stood at the lip of the cave, the new day beginning to break. He was physically tired but mentally alert, his mind closed to all other thoughts. This was it, the time had come.

Terry held out the bell and struck it hard. The distinct note shattered the early morning stillness with a clear ringing sound resonating across the valley.

The seconds passed with agonising slowness, as once more it faded and died on the wind. For a moment there was nothing. Then they heard it. Away in the distance, above the noise of the water, came a deep rumbling, a heavy rolling sound like horses thundering across country.

Terry turned to face the others. But no-one spoke as the sound grew louder and nearer, driving down the gorge, across the rocks and towards the cave. Then it was upon them, an almighty rumbling all around the mouth of the cavern.

Then abruptly it was gone. Silence. All was still. Too still. They exchanged nervous glances. Terry opened his mouth to speak but his words were lost as a great wind whipped up as if from nowhere and tore into the cave. They were thrown backwards by the violent blast as it ripped through the recess, howling like an angry animal, tearing the fire apart and scattering ashes into the air. Cinders and burning wood swirled into the vortex of this preternatural whirlwind spinning like a tornado through the cave. They dropped to the ground for cover as still it went on, dangerous hot embers dancing like fire flies all around them.

And then as suddenly as it had come the wind dropped and died away, leaving sand and fire debris strewn across the cave.

No-one dared move. There was just the hiss of dust settling about them, and the incessant waters rushing by outside.

Terry lowered a protective arm from his head, brushed the hot cinders from his coat and sat up slowly. One by one the others followed, looking around in fear and bewilderment. They stood up cautiously, half expecting the gale to return. But what happened next was something far stranger.

They suddenly heard a mysterious sound, almost like a woman singing, a haunting call drifting on the wind across the valley.

\* \* \* \*

Martin was the first to leave the cave, hoping to trace the source of the eerie sound. He was curious and determined to investigate, but certainly not prepared for what was about to happen. He could not believe his eyes. He blinked and looked again, but it was still there. In the dim twilight of early morning he saw a shimmering white column upon the rocky outcrop about thirty yards away.

He could not begin to imagine what it was, an optical illusion perhaps or a trick of the light. Whether driven by curiosity, some strange foolishness or even the apparition itself, he found himself racing towards it. The others watched as Martin ran along the narrow path and into the gloom. Graham called after him but he had disappeared round the corner of the cliff and out of sight. They followed after him, Terry insisting that Jean and Susan stay in the cave in case there was any danger.

Martin slowed down to an apprehensive walk on nearing the light. He stopped dead at the foot of the rock and stood dumbfounded. 'It can't be, it just can't be,' he repeated to himself. But it was, for there, on the outcrop of rock some ten feet away, was the shimmering human form of a woman in long flowing robes standing motionless, staring down at him from the rock.

A great surge of fear and complete disbelief jarred through his body. This was something completely unnatural, something that should not be. Although the woman stood clearly and unmistakeably before him, less than four yards away, he could still not believe his eyes.

* * * *

Graham, Joe, Mike and Terry stood in amazement as they watched Martin walking apprehensively up the slope towards a white figure standing on the rock. A woman dressed in a long robe which moved and rippled in the breeze.

* * * *

A surreal calm suddenly overcame Martin as he faced the woman and he took a step forward. He was no longer afraid. In some way his mind seemed suddenly to have accepted the unacceptable, and time seemed to almost slow down, even stand still as he stood before her. Strange thoughts went through his mind, a tangle of conscious and unconscious questions and answers.

She was about six feet tall, with long red hair and strangely beautiful. Her white robe hung on a powerful but graceful body and her facial features were almost oriental.

He was transfixed, gazing in awe, wondering what was happening. Then she spoke, strange words in a soft lyrical tongue he had never heard before, but somehow the words became his own native language, translated in his mind.

**'The Stone you seek is not at this place. Be patient. Soon you will know. I will help you.'**

Then he knew. The figure before him was the Celtic Queen Gwevaraugh. Martin fell to his knees, not out of reverence or fear but from a strange sense of weakness. It seemed as if the apparition was drawing energy from him, but when he looked up she was gone, and he was alone on the rock.

When the luminosity faded and the figure disappeared the others ran forward. Martin stared up at them from the ground. 'Did you see her?' he asked.

They had. 'We saw her alright,' answered Graham. 'As clear as day.'

* * * *

They made their way back to the cave and, as Martin recovered from his extraordinary experience, discussed the bizarre event. Jean and Susan were disappointed at not having seen the woman, while Joe, Mike, Terry and Graham were as amazed as Martin. They had stood rooted to the spot as he ran towards the woman and appeared to speak to her. Joe was badly shaken. His long wait through the night had been rewarded, but in a way which questioned his very conception of reality.

The long cold night was over, and in numbed silence they left the cave and made their way back along the dew covered valley.

The spirit of Gwevaraugh had risen.

## Chapter Eight

# Nightmare

The wind wove strange and intricate patterns through the long grass and the hedgerows murmured with tiny insects. Skylarks hovered overhead, singing clearly then dropping like stones into the meadows below. All the while the sun shone brightly in the clear blue sky. The children played beside the narrow winding brook dividing the cattle pastures from the wheat fields, running back and forth along the river bank.

The little blonde girl, Nerys Sunderland, left the chase as her friends ran ahead, her attention caught by a dragonfly skimming across the water. Away down the path she heard the others laughing and shouting. But there was another sound. A whispering voice rising above the noise of the stream. She looked around but saw no-one; she was alone. She knelt and peered curiously at the brook, the waters rippling over the moss covered rocks beneath the surface. The sound must have come from the water washing against the banks.

Forgetting the sound she turned to leave, to chase after the others calling her name downstream. But something else called her name too, a soft whisper came across the waters. She looked up and down the opposite bank. No-one was there, nothing but the tangle of trees, their branches arching over the brook bowing together as if they had come to drink.

Again the voice called. Holding up her hand to shade her eyes from the strong sun breaking through the leaves she saw a white figure, it made her gasp and she stared in fascination. A woman in a long white dress was standing on the opposite bank a short way from the water's edge, but the bright sunlight streaming from behind and catching the mist from the foaming waters prevented a clear view of her face. All she could distinguish was her hair blowing gently in the breeze rising from the cool stream below.

Nerys felt strange. 'Who is it?' she said, feeling frightened and beginning to back away.

'Do not be afraid,' answered the woman, stepping foward so that Nerys could at last see her clearly. The child was transfixed.

* * * *

Graham and Susan arrived at the Sunderland's around 8.00 p.m. on Sunday 8th August. Terry, Pat and Alan were already there. Marion had called them over to explain how something very important had occurred.

'What's happened?' Graham asked Terry, as Marion was upstairs putting the children to bed.

'No idea, but whatever it is Marion looks better.'

'Yes,' said Graham. But he didn't really agree. True, she looked a bit happier, but more like someone putting on a brave face than someone in good health. She was still pale and drawn, and seemed to have lost weight. Her eyes were sunken and dark ringed and she was trembling as she collected the coffee mugs. He had not seen her for a fortnight, but Terry had visited her the previous Monday to explain what happened in the Dove Valley. Graham wanted to know how she had been then.

Terry glanced round to check she was out of ear shot. 'Terrible,' he whispered. 'She was obviously disappointed and as confused as we were about what happened. But there was something more, I'm sure of it.' They fell quiet as Marion came in with more coffee. Everyone sat round, eagerly awaiting her news.

'I think someone's trying to help us,' said Marion.

'Who?' asked Alan.

'A woman in white appeared and spoke to Nerys.'

'Where?'

'By the brook across the fields.' Marion explained how her youngest daughter Nerys had been out playing with friends when someone had called her. A woman in white standing by the stream.

'She told Nerys to fetch her mother and return as quickly as possible.'

'What happened? Was Nerys frightened?' asked Pat.

'A bit. I thought it was someone trying to scare her so I told her to stay in the house and went on my own. But there was no-one there. When I got back, Nerys wasn't frightened anymore and asked me if she could return. Apparently the woman needed her there too. The more I thought about it the more I began to feel there was something genuinely supernatural about it. But I still didn't like the idea of Nerys going back. Well, that was yesterday. Then last night I was about to go to bed when Nerys came downstairs and said she'd seen the woman in her bedroom. I ran upstairs but there was no-one there.'

'Could she have dreamt it?' asked Pat.

'I suppose so, but as she wasn't scared anymore I told her to ask the woman what she wanted if she appeared again. This morning, when the others were out, she said the lady had returned and told her.'

'What? Who was she' asked Graham.

Marion picked up a notepad from the sideboard. 'I wrote it all down. She told Nerys she had a message for me, and that I must not worry. She was there to help us but we had to be patient.'

'She sounds like the same lady we saw at Ilam Rock.' Terry said.

Marion nodded. 'She told Nerys that she had spoken to Martin and told her exactly what she said to him. As you know Nerys knew nothing about what happened at Ilam Rock.'

They discussed this intriguing turn of events, trying to decide what to do next.

'Why don't we try and speak to Gwevaraugh again,' said Susan.

'How?' asked Graham.

'Go with Nerys to where she first saw her,' Alan said.

But Marion rightly did not wish to involve Nerys any further in case she became frightened, and volunteered to go herself instead.

'I'm sure we don't need to actually go to a particular place,' said Pat. 'She's already appeared in the house and can presumably do so again.'

Pat went on to suggest that perhaps now the time was right for them to obtain further psychic information in the same way as before, by sitting round in a circle. After some discussion they agreed to make an attempt. Marion was still reluctant to include Gaynor, who went up to her room as the others sat in a circle on the floor.

'I'd prefer it if we left the light on,' said Marion as Terry reached out to flick the switch. She was plainly still upset by the dreadful experience at Ranton.

All was silent for some minutes before Pat spoke, 'I think I can feel something.' She shivered and rubbed her arms. 'I don't like it.' At that moment Marion suddenly burst into tears. 'I don't understand what's happening,' she sobbed. 'It feels as if ... ' when suddenly and without warning Gaynor rushed into the room.

'Stop it,' she shouted. 'For God's sake stop it.'

They stared at her in astonishment. 'We mustn't try to

communicate. There's something else here. Something's terribly wrong.'

* * * *

Marion sat alone in her living room. She could not understand what was happening to her, she just could not cope any more. The nights were worst. She would fall asleep dog tired, only to wake up ten minutes later shaking and sweating with fear, as if something dreadful had happened. She would lie awake for hours, too frightened to relax, then eventually drift into a fitful sleep, but after no time at all she had to get up to see the children off to school. During the day the slightest problem would bring her to the brink of tears, and though she endeavoured not to let the children see her so distressed it was becoming increasingly difficult to hide her emotions. She was sure they had noticed. Still more disturbing was her state of health, she had back pains, sickness and headaches. She could not imagine what was wrong with her.

The doctor said she was run down and in need of a rest. He booked her in for a check-up at the local hospital where they diagnosed a slight kidney infection and prescribed a course of tablets. But this did not explain everything. Her ill-health had begun immediately after her confrontation at Ranton Abbey. Marion still shuddered whenever she thought about it. It was as if something had disturbed her very soul.

Since that day she had experienced the unshakeable feeling that something horrible was nearby, watching her and waiting.

Now she was alone. The children were at school and Fred was away again with the Territorial Army. It was the first time she had been on her own in the house since it had all begun. She wanted desperately to rush out, to be with other people, but she refused to give in to what she felt were ungrounded fears. After all she was perfectly safe, there could be nothing in the house, nothing out to do her harm. She sank back in the chair and relaxed, closing her eyes and willing herself to relax.

The noise came from above, punching her mind back to wakefulness. Something had moved, upstairs, it sounded as if someone had walked heavily across her bedroom above.

The muscles in her chest tightened and she bit her lip. Her heart raced as she strained her ears and gripped the arms of the chair.

But now everything was still, and the only noise was the traffic passing along the coast road at the end of the close. The seconds ticked by agonisingly, but nothing happened. So she stood up cautiously, her eyes glued to the ceiling overhead, there was still no sound and she relaxed slightly. Perhaps it had been a noise from next door, the water pipes or the floor timbers contracting. She waited, half hoping to hear the sound again so she could identify it and dismiss it from her mind. But all was silent, and Marion reproached herself for being so stupid. She decided to investigate just to be on the safe side.

She left the room and climbed the stairs, smiling at the familiar creaking underfoot as she did so. Her bedroom and all the other rooms were empty. She heaved a sigh of relief, returned downstairs and made herself a cup of coffee. Five minutes later she had almost forgotten the incident, absent-mindedly watching the television and wondering what to give the children for dinner.

She jumped involuntarily, coffee spilling everywhere, as the noise came again. It was a series of heavy thuds, about two seconds apart, as if someone was pounding slowly and deliberately across the floor above. She sprang up and switched off the television, straining her ears to catch the sound clearly, but it had stopped. She toyed with the idea of running to fetch a neighbour but quickly decided against it. She would just look silly. There had to be a simple explanation. She wondered if there was someone upstairs, but that was impossible, she had already checked.

She sat back in the armchair and waited. If it came again she would just have to work out what it was.

Marion almost leapt out of her seat as a shrill double tone filled the room. She laughed aloud, it was only the cuckoo clock. But her laughter was short lived, giving way to cold fear as the noise began again. Now it was different though, two slow and powerful steps across the bedroom floor, a pause, followed by a deep rumbling vibration like heavy machinery reverberating through the house. This time there was no doubt about it, the noises were in the house, in the bedroom, right above her. There was no way it could be a heavy lorry in the distant traffic. The whole ceiling was vibrating, the light fitting shaking and beginning to swing.

Marion wondered if it was an earth tremor and the thought temporarily calmed her. It certainly could be that, they had happened in North Wales before, and it would explain the vibration. **But not the footsteps**.

The noise stopped, and she waited in silence, hardly realising she was holding her breath, causing her heart to beat even louder. She exhaled, but then the dull thud struck again above her. She sat absolutely still, staring in fear at the ceiling. A second loud thud, and then a third. A fourth, they were getting louder, moving across the bedroom towards the door. A long pace every two or three seconds. She sat in the armchair, close to panic, simply waiting for it to stop. But the footsteps continued and this time they did not stop. She sat petrified, unable to move. The whole place felt electrified, the hairs stood up on the back of her neck and goose pimples raised on her arms. The footsteps had left the bedroom and were crossing the landing, heading for the staircase. She had to get out, now and quickly.

Then an awful realisation dawned on her, she could not move a muscle. It was not like straining against an invisible force, her limbs simply refused to react to the commands from her brain. She could hardly **feel** her body.

The footsteps continued, slowly and irrevocably across the landing and towards the top of the stairs. They came nearer and nearer. Marion tried again desperately to move, but it was as if she were paralysed, apart from her head and neck the terrifying cataleptic state held the rest of her body completely immobile.

By now the footsteps had reached the head of the stairs. Suddenly they stopped and there was silence. Marion held her breath, terrified that they would begin again. Ten, twenty, thirty seconds passed like long hours but still it was quiet. Then she thought she heard the floorboards creak at the top of the stairs. The familiar giveaway sound when one of the children was out of bed, but Marion knew she was alone in the house. Alone yet someone, or something, was at the top of the stairs. **Waiting**.

She struggled frantically to move, but still her limbs refused to respond and by now she had broken into a cold sweat. Her heart was beating so loudly that she could actually hear it quite clearly. She twisted and turned her head from side to side. **Please. Let me move. Please**.

Then there was another footfall. Not so loud, but it was on the stairs, followed by another thud. **Oh God, it's coming downstairs**. Something heavy and solid pounded onto each step, the floorboards creaking beneath its weight. She opened her mouth to scream, but no sound came. Just a harsh whisper, her vocal chords were frozen in sheer terror.

'**Help. Help. Please ... somebody help me.**' Her strangled cries were barely audible. No-one would hear and she knew it.

The footsteps continued, they were now halfway down the staircase.

With great effort she managed to turn her body and twist her neck to look out of the window. A passerby might happen to glance in and see her anguished face, and realise she needed help. But the street was deserted and seemed strangely dark for mid afternoon. Heavy black thunderclouds scudded overhead, threatening to open into a deluge at any moment.

The footsteps continued relentlessly. **FIVE STAIRS TO GO**. In helpless anguish she had counted each one, she knew the exact number. **NOW FOUR**.

In mortal dread Marion knew that whatever was coming toward her could not be human. She had after all checked everywhere upstairs; all the rooms, under the beds and even the cupboards. No-one could have been hiding and remained undiscovered.

### THREE

And she could not move. Whatever it was it had numbed her body, rendering her powerless and unable to escape its inexorable approach.

### TWO

At last she knew. The terrible feelings of the past few weeks, the fear always there just below the surface of her mind, had been something following and watching her, waiting for the right moment, which was when she was alone in the house, then it could come for her.

### ONE

The footsteps touched the last stair, and there was deathly silence. It was now just outside, with only the living room door between her and …

Outside the sky seemed suddenly even darker. Marion sat transfixed in the gloom, horrified. The familiar interior of the living room was strangely altered by the unnatural twilight, it was now a dangerous and menacing place of threatening shadows and mysterious objects. The air was icy, she felt so cold and there was mist on her breath as she exhaled.

She could no longer struggle, only sit where she was, bound in terror, staring at the door, thinking her heart might burst from her body it was pounding so hard. She could do nothing but stare at the door and wait for the inevitable.

It became clear in her mind like a ghastly realisation erupting from her subconscious, crystalising the reason for her constant feeling of alarm ever since they had fled from Ranton Abbey. The Ranton Guardian had not been laid to rest when they found the bell. It was not confined to Ranton Abbey, not even the proximity of the bell. She had known this really at the moment she had faced it with the strength of her own will, when for a split second it was as if she and the Guardian were one. As she had left the Abbey Marion had sensed that the Guardian was like a dangerous but wounded animal, and it had been injured by her. Now she knew that once it recovered it would seek out and destroy its assailant, and this was it. The thing behind the door had come for her.

The handle slowly moved and the door began to open. A freezing blast of air filled the room. Her skin crawled and sweat poured from her brow as she struggled desperately to escape. Overcome by blind terror and incomprehension she watched helplessly as the door opened wide. Marion froze and stared in abject horror.

In the doorway was a naked human, pale and grey skinned. Its hair danced and swayed as if surrounded by a powerful static field. An emotionless face stared her cold in the eyes. She recognised it immediately, the second the door opened.

Too late, Marion understood exactly what was happening. She should have known, should have realised before, for now, not only she but all of them would be destroyed.

The creature that stood before her was a bizarre duplicate of herself.

Marion screamed as the darkness closed in and consciousness drifted from her mind.

## Chapter Nine
# Something in the House

'So she either passed out and came to a while later, or she'd fallen asleep and dreamt the whole thing,' concluded Alan, after explaining what had happened to Marion.

'What do you think?' Terry said.

'I honestly don't know. Marion can't be sure. She said the whole thing was so completely unreal, and after what happened at Ranton, and her poor state of health, it could have been just a nightmare.'

'How was she last night?' Terry asked, with ever growing concern.

'Very frightened. She thinks that, even if it was only a terrible dream, we're all in great danger.'

'Why?'

'She doesn't seem to know. Just before she saw that the manifestation was herself, she realised something. But try as she might she can't remember what. She's convinced it's very important though.'

In the living room of the Shotton's Staffordshire cottage Terry and Alan talked well into the evening, discussing Marion's disturbing experience and the strange course of events since the discovery of the Bell.

They pondered whether Marion had fallen asleep in her armchair, and if so was it significant apart from being an indication of her general state of mind following her trauma at Ranton. She was certain that the Guardian was responsible for her terrifying ordeal, whether it was a nightmare or a supernatural manifestation. Thankfully five days had now elapsed and nothing further had occurred. So perhaps she was wrong to conclude it had been the Guardian.

At 10.30 that evening Pat returned from visiting relatives with their two children Neil and Joanne. She put them to bed and began preparing supper. Outside the wind was rising.

'We can't deny that the Guardian **did** exist,' said Terry. 'We all saw what happened at Ranton. But surely if it still exists it's either confined to the Abbey or attached to the Bell. Graham's got the bell and nothing's happened to him.'

Alan shrugged. 'Perhaps you ought to phone him.'

Terry agreed. Graham had in fact already spoken to Marion and knew of the latest events. He had reached the same conclusion as Terry, and he confirmed that all was quiet with him.

'I think we should all quit,' said Alan when Terry had finished on the telephone, 'Give it up and forget the Red Stone.'

Pat was in full agreement, she felt it was getting out of hand. Terry understood her concern, particularly for the children, and knew that Alan had for some time been close to the limit of his endurance. Ranton had been the last straw which was why Alan could not bring himself to go into the Dove Valley two weeks before. Now, after what happened to Marion, he'd had enough. Terry was about to agree with his wife and Alan. Curiosity had been his motive in their strange adventure, but he was growing ever more mindful of the old adage about curiosity.

And then something happened.

The wind blew fiercely outside, rattling the window frames and bowling over a dustbin round the back, sending it clattering noisily across the yard. The telegraph wires, whining overhead, pitched higher at the sudden ferocity of the gale then fell silent as the wind suddenly dropped. All became still out in the night. The three stopped talking, alerted by the distinct change. They all felt it independently, a subtle twist in the atmosphere, the peculiar feeling of suspension awaiting an impending event, as if something was just about to happen. And it did, suddenly there was a loud bang on the front door. They froze, until Terry stood up slowly. They weren't expecting anyone.

'You'd better take a look,' said Pat hesitantly.

Terry went to the window and drew back the curtain, cupping his hand over his eyes to get a better view. 'There's no-one there,' he said.

Alan and Terry went to the front door and opened it. The rough trackway that led to the cottage was lonely and deserted. No-one was anywhere in sight. The only sign of life came from the lights from the cottages and bungalows along the lane. All was still, but a fine drizzle had begun to fall. It was all too quiet.

Alan was about to speak when a blast of freezing air hit them both hard in the face, it was bitterly cold, colder than the surrounding air, yet no wind was blowing outside.

In the living room Pat called out to ask what they had found, when suddenly the door to the hall flew open and a wintry blast tore through the room. The curtains blew wildly and papers were lifted from the table. Terry and Alan ran back in as the fearsome wind receded as quickly as it had come.

It had left the room so cold.

'What's happening?' Pat asked incredulously.

Terry closed the door and leant back against it. He looked at Pat then stared at Alan who was white faced and shaking. 'I don't know,' he said slowly. 'Is the back door open?'

Pat shook her head. 'No.'

'A window?'

They knew there wasn't. The wind could not have ripped through the room so viciously.

'Terry!' Alan's voice was a harsh and desperate whisper, he was staring toward the door. 'There's someone in the hall.'

Pat stood up and backed away as the door began to open. It was her daughter.

'Joanne,' said Pat with relief. Joanne stood shivering in her nightdress, tears running down her cheeks, eyes wide and afraid.

'There's something in the house,' she said quietly.

* * * *

The young girl walked swiftly down the lane as the trees rustled in the night and a thin layer of cloud veiled the quarter moon. She never looked forward to leaving her boyfriend on the bus at the end of the village, but the walk down the muddy track to her home she liked even less. There were no street lamps to guide the way, only the occasional porch light from the few houses set fifty yards or so back from the patchy hedgerows to either side. Her parents always told her never to walk alone after dark through the city streets. She always agreed but often disobeyed. Muggings, rape and all the rest, no-one ever thinks it will happen to them. Here in the rural night there existed a strange paradox of fear, here you always think it **will** be you.

As she passed the short row of cottages at the bend in the lane before turning into her own driveway, something made her stop. She felt a strange sensation. She was almost home, the creepy lane behind her, but she couldn't go on. She was too afraid. There was something ahead of her. She could not bring herself to pass the end cottage. The air around was cold, like walking into an icy hollow. She stood staring at the house. The downstairs lights were on. She knew the people who lived there, the Shottons, they were probably watching T.V. Everything seemed quite normal, so what, she wondered, was wrong. As she looked at the upstairs windows her flesh began to creep. The lights were out, but an eerie blue glow flickered and pulsated through the open curtains, intermittently illuminating the walls and furnishings of the bedroom. A strange configuration of lines like glowing cracks began to appear on the window panes.

She turned and fled.

* * * *

There had been an unexplained knock at the front door. Followed by an inexplicable gust of wind which tore through the house, then a strange unnatural chill in the air. They could not explain what had happened at the Shotton's home that Saturday evening.

Joanne had woken from a disturbed sleep with the terrifying feeling that something horrible had entered the cottage. Alan also felt it and left immediately, too afraid to stay any longer.

Over the next few days Terry and Pat tried to dismiss the disturbing occurrence from their minds and continue their every day lives. But the strange events continued. The living room would frequently become bitterly cold for no apparent reason, and they would be forced to light a fire in the grate, even though the summer sun was shining brightly outside. Peculiar pungent odours would waft through the upstairs bedrooms whether the windows were open or closed, and household objects would move without explanation.

Not only the Shottons but visitors to the cottage also witnessed these unnerving phenomena. People who knew nothing of the strange events said they felt very uncomfortable in the house but were unable to explain why. Particularly odd was that a passerby on the night it began, a neighbour's daughter, had not only felt the uncanny sensation surrounding the place but had also seen an eerie blue light in the window of Terry and Pat's bedroom. Had the Saverley Green cottage suddenly become haunted? It certainly seemed so. This was disturbing enough but Terry harboured an even greater fear. Had the Guardian come for **him**? After all he was the one who found and removed the Bell. If so what could he do? Then an idea occured to him, perhaps if he returned the bell to Ranton he could put things right.

On Wednesday evening he travelled across to Marion's to discuss the situation and put forward his idea. He was shocked to see the extend to which Marion's health had deteriorated. She was even more pale and withdrawn, but she agreed with Terry's suggestion,

Martin Keatman (left) and Graham Phillips (right).

Brinklow Hill.

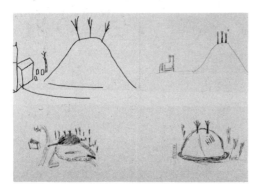

The psychic drawings of Brinklow Hill made independently by four people during the seance of 20th March, 1982.

From left to right: Nerys, Marion and Gaynor Sunderland.

David and Sheila Bavington.

The ruined lodge at Ranton, haunted by a terrible curse that
almost claimed their lives.

Graham Philips stands beneath the archway at Ranton where the Bell was discovered.

The living room in the Shotton's cottage. From left to right: Mike Ratcliffe, Joanne, Terry and Pat Shotton, Janet Morgan and Joe Larosa.

Jean stands at the entrance to the cave in Dovedale.

The rock in Dovedale Gorge where the lady in white miraculously appeared before them.

St. Bennet's Abbey on the Norfolk Broads. Within these ancient walls, lay a secret message, the ultra-clue in their search to gain the priceless red stone.

The Boat that took them on the perilous voyage to discover The Eye of Fire.

JOHN MERRON

'A tall black figure stood motionless at the waters edge, drenched in swirling grey mist.' Picture taken of the Abbey at dawn on 19th September, 1982, as Terry Shotton prepared to meet his death.

Janet Morgan next to the **Well of Sacred Blood** in the old orchard at Saverley Green.

The Bell, discovered so dramatically in the
crumbling walls at Ranton Lodge.

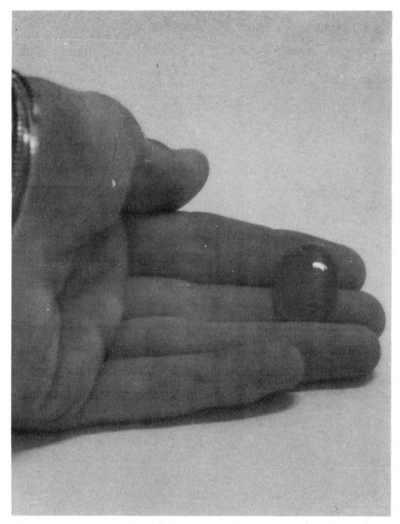

The Eye of Fire.

The disturbing photograph taken of Brinklow Hill on 16th September, 1982, in which a strange dark figure in Victorian clothes mysteriously appeared on film.

Enlargement of above. A ghost photographed on Brinklow Hill?

after all they had nothing to lose. The only problem was who would take it back. Needless to say no-one relished the prospect. Gaynor, however, took the decision for them. She said that not only would it do no good, but that it would be extremely dangerous.

Terry was not sure of this but had no intention of finding out and decided to take her word for it.

'There must be something we can do,' he said.

'I'm sorry,' said Gaynor, 'I honestly don't know.'

When Terry returned home that night he was extremely concerned. The house was empty. Pat was at a church meeting and the children were staying with their grandmother. The uninviting cold atmosphere seemed worse than ever and he set about lighting a fire.

Just after 11.00 p.m. he heard the first noise, a strange scraping sound somewhere above him. He looked up from the fire and listened. It came again, a prolonged, muffled sound like something being dragged across the floor somewhere upstairs. Terry's first impulse was to run from the house. His nerves were already on edge and now his stomach began to churn. 'Pull yourself together,' he muttered and trying to convince himself it was probably an airlock in the pipes, he decided to check it out. He went into the hallway, switched on the landing light and stood at the bottom of the staircase.

'Anyone upstairs?' he called, the sound of his own voice normalising the strange atmosphere. He had just reached the top when the noise came again, from the direction of his bedroom at the opposite end of the landing. There was a dull thud. The bedroom door was ajar and he could see through into the dark interior.

'I know it's just the pipes,' he said, loudly, and continued talking to himself as he walked briskly across the landing. Switching on the light he edged slowly into the bedroom. It was empty. Of course it was. So where had the noise come from? His thoughts were answered by a deep rumbling sound as if something heavy was being pulled across the loft above him. Terry knew full well that there could be no natural explanation. He listened in petrified silence as the sound continued over the length of the ceiling from one side to the other. There could be no mistake, the noise was only two feet above his head.

His legs felt weak and there was a sinking feeling in the pit of his stomach. Terry began to back out of the room when the noise stopped with one last dull thud. The light bulb in the bedroom flared up brightly and shattered, plunging him into darkness.

A deep sigh came from somewhere in the room.

# Chapter Ten
# Psychic Fury

Something had to be done to stop these horrifying assaults. Marion was terrified beyond endurance, her health continued to deteriorate and the Shottons were being driven from their home.

As Terry and Graham discussed their frightening predicament in the earthy surroundings of Saverley Green's village pub, both knew that time was running out. The odds were stacked high against them. The only hope was to reason it out and try to understand what they were up against.

Both Marion and Gaynor were convinced that the distressing turn of events since the dramatic discovery at Ranton were caused by the Guardian. Terry was equally certain when he investigated the strange noise in his bedroom the previous evening and the light bulb had mysteriously blown, that he was not alone. He not only heard the impossible disembodied breathing but felt its presence. It only lasted a moment, but he recognised both the sound and the sensation. The same awful foreboding as that evening at Ranton Abbey.

Graham had to agree with Terry. It did seem likely that their invisible assailant was what they had been calling the Guardian, but what was the Guardian? Something ultimately beyond their understanding. A paranormal creation which was the controlling force behind a series of nightmarish phenomena that could create just about any fear imaginable. How much was illusion and how much physical reality was impossible to tell. From what they had witnessed so far there could be no doubt that it **was** capable of affecting solid matter. In other words it posed a very real danger to mind **and** body.

Gaynor had told them something about the Guardian, and they could only accept she was right. Mary Heath had brought it into existence by using The Eye of Fire, an ancient Red Stone that could amplify the psychic powers of the unconscious mind. She had created a venomous being, an extension of her own will to guard the only clue to the location of the Stone. Mary's intention was to stop John Laing from gaining possession of the bell, but should he do so, to destroy him before he discovered its secret. According to Gaynor, Mary would not have wished harm to them but the Guardian was a programmed entity, blindly following its original instructions.

Graham now had the bell though nothing disturbing was happening to him. The malevolence seemed to be directed only at Marion and Terry, so the answer must have something to do with Mary's thoughts when she created the Guardian. It was created with Laing in mind, and it must surely have been her intention to give it the means to defend itself against any adverse occult influence. Marion had tried to stand against it and now it was striking back. The Guardian must also have been 'programmed' to destroy whoever found the bell, unless it was the person she had intended to find it. Considering the short time available this was presumably the only way Mary could protect her secret without exposing many innocent people to the destructive curse.

Terry now appeared to be its intended victim, and they did not know how to protect him. Returning the bell, Gaynor told them, would not only be futile but dangerous. It seemed things were growing steadily worse. They could not afford to ignore it and cling onto the vague hope that it would all go away. Their only chance now was to find The Eye of Fire so that maybe it could destroy the Guardian.

Gwevaraugh, the strange apparition, had said she could help, but so far had done nothing, and their further attempts to communicate with her had all failed.

They needed desperately to gain time. With Marion's deteriorating health and Terry's worsening plight, how could they be protected until they could discover the secret of the bell.

'I can only think of one thing,' said Graham. 'It seems that the Guardian is like a dangerous animal. Perhaps that's the way Mary Heath envisaged it, as a sort of psychic guard dog. Wounded by Marion at Ranton it's recovered, found her scent and tracked her down. Now it's found you, the one who invaded its lair'.

Terry shook visibly. 'How does that help?' he said.

'We don't know how to destroy it, but maybe we could snare it.'

'How?' said Terry.

'We might be able to envelope it in a sort of psychic net.' Graham went on, explaining his theory.

Two years previously Gaynor had received a psychic message about an isolated pool near Terry's house in Saverley Green where people had witnessed unexplained phenomena. She said it was a place once revered by ancient peoples since it held a strange power. She called it the Pool of Protection.

'If we can assume Gaynor is right,' Graham said. 'Perhaps we can use it to trap the Guardian.'

'How?'

'It's a long shot I know, but we could simply go there and concentrate our minds on raising a force to envelope the Guardian.'

Terry agreed it was better than nothing. 'How do we make sure the Guardian is there?' he asked.

'Well it seems to be after you, so unfortunately you're the bait.'

Terry smiled wryly. 'Thanks.'

\* \* \* \*

On Saturday, 21st August, nine people joined Terry and Pat at the cottage. Joe, Mike, Jean, Alan, Marion, Gaynor, Graham, Susan and Chris Bourne, a friend of Terry's who had offered to help.

It had not been at all easy to persuade Marion to come, but Terry had eventually convinced her it was their only hope. Still something nagged at the back of her mind, making her reluctant, she did not know why but she felt unsure about it.

Although the night was warm, a fire blazed in the grate to stave off the uncanny chill in the small cottage. They sat around as Graham explained his plan of action. They would go to the pool and stand in a circle as Terry and Marion called upon the Guardian.

'It's all I can think of,' he said. 'If the minds of those the Guardian seeks are concentrating totally on it perhaps it will respond.'

'Then what do we do?' asked Alan.

'Once either Marion or Terry senses its presence the rest of us must concentrate the full power of our minds on the single thought of raising the force of protection from the pool. We then imagine we are enveloping the Guardian with the same power. We might succeeed in trapping it, holding it there.'

'Do you think it will work?' Alan said, directing his question at Gaynor.

'I don't know,' she said, 'but the pool is a powerful psychic place.'

'I admit it sounds pretty far fetched,' continued Graham, 'but we can't deny what's been happening and how right Gaynor's been in the past. If she thinks that some kind of protective power can be raised there I'm prepared to give it a go.'

Alan still looked worried. 'Even if Gaynor is right,' he said, 'and we are able to summon the Guardian what makes you so sure we can hold it there.'

'I'm not sure,' admitted Graham, but he explained his theory. For centuries right across the world, holy men, mystics and occultists believed in the power of the magic circle, a ring of pyschic power that the magician cast about himself for protection from evil influences. This could be achieved in many different ways, but the basic principle was always the same. Once the circle of protection was created nothing supernatural could pass in or out, although the magician, a physical being, would be unaffected and could come and go at will.

'The magic circle was normally used to keep things out, but it also worked the other way,' concluded Graham.

'Do we have to go across to the pool?' asked Marion, visibly showing her alarm. 'Can't we do it somewhere less isolated first of all?'

'We could,' interjected Terry, 'but I don't think it's advisable.' If they did manage to call the Guardian they might have only one chance. They must be sure they could call upon a protective power at that time. The pool was the only place they knew. No-one liked the idea, especially in the dark, but if they went ahead it would have to be at night. Gaynor emphasised that daylight would negatively influence not only the Guardian's appearance, but the protective power itself. Unfortunately she could offer no further explanation for this.

By 9.45 p.m. the last light of day faded from the evening sky and the decision was made. They would have to try. Marion insisted that Gaynor stay in the house and Joe, Chris and Jean remained with her.

As the seven of them climbed the garden fence and disappeared across the dark fields, those remaining in the cottage could only hope and pray that everything would be all right.

\* \* \* \*

Marion felt terribly concerned as she tried to remember. It was there, just below the surface of her mind. She had found out something about the Guardian that awful day it had entered her living-room, but now the knowledge had gone.

The night was mild and the sky clear. The fields buzzed with the sound of crickets as the sweet smell of freshly cut grass drifted on the cool refreshing breeze. The ancient hawthorn rows joined the lines of oak and rowan forming a dark garland of mysterious shapes which bordered the broad meadows. The huddled silhouettes moved silently across the moonlit pastures as the twinkling lights of the tiny hamlet receded into the distance, seven friends drawing closer to the silent and lonely pool. Crossing the last ditch and crawling under the barbed wire fence where it encircled an old withered yew, Terry halted and gazed ahead across the field.

'That's it,' he said, pointing to a clump of tall trees set against the skyline. The others bunched up behind him. Marion leant against a fence post to catch her breath.

'I don't think I can go through with it,' she said.

Everyone knew that Marion was unwell, even their leisurely pace had left her weak and trembling.

'Come on,' said Terry. There was no point in delaying the inevitable.

They filed across the grass, following the beam of Terry's torch until they arrived at the two stone pillars marking the end of the journey. Grey weathered stones erected long ago to mark the boundary of some ancient estate. Recently they had served as gate posts, and a double line of barbed wire ran between them. Terry held the wires apart as his friends climbed through one by one and followed Pat into the dark copse.

At the heart of the broad circle of beech and dying elms nestled the algae covered pond, quite quiet in the summer night. Weeping willows hung low and heavy over the stagnant waters. Susan was the last through the wire, and she and Terry cast a final glance back towards the direction of the cottage, then joined the others at the edge of the pool.

'We may as well get started,' said Graham, ushering the others into a circle.

A thin white cloud partly obscured the moon and a soft breeze rustled through the surrounding greenery. At Graham's suggestion they linked hands. A sheep bleeted away in the distance and a second answered nearby. Marion and Terry began to concentrate. Everyone knew they were playing with fire, but they were convinced there was no alternative. There was certainly no going back now.

An icy tremor ran over Marion's flesh at the thought of what they were doing. She recalled that day at Ranton Abbey, standing in the crumbling ruin, and felt sure they should not be taking such a perilous risk. Somehow she knew, but could find no reason to counsel the others, and only with great reluctance had she agreed. If only she could remember. Maybe even now it was not too late.

Terry glanced at the others, dark shapes looking about him, waiting for something to happen. Marion motionless, her head bowed in concentration. He closed his eyes and summoned every

last ounce of his will. He shivered as he mentally forced the words
'Guardian come to me.'

* * * *

Back at the cottage Gaynor sat in silence beside the fire next to
Chris. Jean and Joe sat quietly at the dining room table. It was quite
still outside. Gaynor shivered and drew nearer the fire, her body still
aware of the chilling atmosphere in the house.

But it was more than that, there was an oppressive brooding
malevolence around them. Then something began to change. She
looked up from the comforting flames of the fire and across the
room. Chris had noticed it too. He rubbed his shoulders and glanced
behind him. Then, for a moment, the lights dimmed and a shrill hiss
came from somewhere above them.

Suddenly the peculiar feeling that Gaynor had felt since entering
the cottage began to fade. The light brightened again and the noise
stopped, the atmosphere had altered. Then Gaynor knew what it
was. Something had left the house.

* * * *

Graham's arm was almost yanked from its socket as Marion pulled
at his hand. 'It's coming,' she hissed, 'I can feel it.'

'Are you sure?'

'Positive, Terry can you feel it?'

Terry was about to speak when a loud squawk came from behind
him. Their hearts almost missed a beat as a bird shot out from the
reeds on the opposite side of the pond, wings beating loudly as it
rose into the air.

Terry muttered a jovial curse of relief and the others began to
laugh. But Marion quickly silenced them. 'It's here,' she said.

A single unbroken note jarred their nerves and pierced the
night.

Alan turned to run. 'Don't break the circle,' screamed Pat.

'Graham!' cried Terry, 'what do we do.'

'Er ... concentrate ... try to ...'

'Envelope it!' yelled Pat.

'How?' pleaded Terry.

The noise screamed across the pool, growing louder all the time.
Terry craned his neck to look behind him. A painful vibration struck
him hard in the face, and he almost fell.

'Don't look, concentrate!' shouted Pat. 'Concentrate ... Envelope
it. Trap it.' Her voice rose in competition with the dreadful sound as

she repeated the words over and over again. 'Envelope it ... Envelope it.' One by one the others joined in, shouting aloud in unison. 'Envelop it. Envelope it!' A bizarre chant, defiantly calling out in the night.

Although they could see nothing in the darkness something was there. They could all feel it. Something threatening and terrible, a black abomination only yards away.

The noise began to rise in pitch, a wailing siren, louder and louder.

Marion felt numb. Her head was dizzy, her legs beginning to give way. Someone held her steady. The chants of her friends faded into a muffled buzz as the terrible noise seemed to absorb her very soul. One thought remained, she ... they must all ... continue ... throw the power of their combined will ... destroy the thing ... hold it ... trap it.

**Oh God No. No!** It was then that she suddenly remembered. The knowledge struck her like a thunderbolt, flooding back into her conscious mind, and with all her remaining strength Marion tore herself free from Mike and Graham and raced away through the trees.

'Run!' she screamed, 'Run! - Run!'

The abominable noise continued unabated, firing towards them across the pool and rising in pitch to an ear shattering crescendo. Alan needed no further encouragement. He was filled with dread. A second later he broke the circle and rushed after Marion, leaving the others stranded in numbed confusion.

Marion stumbled to a halt by the trees as Alan hurtled past her.

'Get out,' she screamed. 'It's feeding on us. RUN!'

'Graham!' Shouted Terry, 'What ...?'

But Graham was gone, closely followed by the rest, tearing across the field away from the infernal Guardian.

'Shit!' cried Terry, and ran like he had never run before.

They tumbled through the barbed wire, not caring if their clothes were torn or the sharp metal ripped into their flesh. They were stricken with total fear, racing for their lives across the field and away from the horror pursuing them. In their confusion and blind panic it was every man for himself.

The evil sound emerged from the waters and rose above the trees, reaching a deafening climax and exploding with a tremendous force. A great flash of blue light flared over the copse, followed by an ear shattering bang and a heavy shock wave that filled the air.

'Down!' yelled Graham. They dropped to the ground like stones and lay spread-eagled on the cold grass as a sickly hot wind blasted over them.

## Chapter Eleven
# Haunted

Gaynor sat in the classroom, sunlight streaming in through the open windows. Particles of dust danced in the golden rays which cast stark shadows from the desks and pupils sitting in neat rows. Outside were the cries of other children on the playing fields, the peep of a whistle and the shouted instructions from the coach as the football team trained for the new season.

Inside the teacher's voice droned on and on about textiles, labour and cottage industries.

Gaynor jotted the occasional note, interspersed with doodles and irrelevant scribble. A lazy late summer afternoon, and not the sort of day for lessons. It was the start of a new term and no-one was in the mood for the rigours of work. She had just decided she would probably be asked the next question when a horrible sensation suddenly gripped her. She was being watched. Looking up from her exercise book she glanced around the classroom. A friend caught her eye and looked skywards in a gesture of boredom. Gaynor smiled, quickly assuming 'eyes front' as the girl's inattentiveness was noticed. But the impression remained, she was sure someone was watching her. After a few moments she looked round again. All eyes were fixed on the blackboard as a map was being chalked on. Roused from her daydreaming Gaynor was alert and a strange feeling of vulnerability seemed to envelope her.

Turning and staring through the window she immediately knew why. Across the playground, beyond the surrounding park, stood a black silhouette upon the high grassy bank bordering the school. Even from a hundred yards away she could feel his malevolent presence. Gaynor sensed he was watching and waiting, for what she did not know.

The disgruntled voice of the school mistress called out her name. She turned, and was asked to explain what was so interesting outside. Gaynor looked again, but the figure was gone. She was about to answer, but there was no point. 'Nothing Miss,' she said.

No one would believe her. The tall dark figure in victorian clothes outside her school was something only she would understand.

* * * *

For three weeks now nothing strange had occured in the Shotton household, and life had returned to an uneasy normality. Terry was still deeply disturbed, he felt it was only a temporary respite. In the last dramatic moments at the pool Marion had discovered the awful truth, or rather she had recalled the peculiar insight she had gained in her house as she faced her bizarre double. The Guardian could not be overcome. It absorbed the power that was thrown against it and simply grew stronger, which explained how Marion had been rendered so weak. The Guardian had drained the psychic energy she had used to try and overcome it. The grotesque facsimile was a duplicated part of her own being, a psychic vampire drawing off her inner strength. As the Guardian had come closer she had remembered, and knew that the power they were raising against it would be absorbed to strengthen it. She was sure that after their attempt to defeat it the Guardian would only be temporarily disabled. Once it recovered it would be stronger than ever, wielding the added potency it had consumed.

They had used the strongest influence they knew but now, when the Guardian returned, there would be no way of fending it off.

They all hoped Marion was wrong for once. Terry could do nothing but beg for time, and pray that the Guardian would not return until they had found the Red Stone. They felt sure the Stone was their only chance of laying it to rest.

* * * *

So far everything had been quiet. It was Saturday, 11 September, and Graham and Martin travelled across to Saverley Green.

'Marion's no better or worse,' concluded Terry, 'but she's obviously still very frightened.'

'Perhaps she's wrong,' said Graham, 'maybe the worst is over.'

'I'd like to think so,' said Terry.

'We may all be over-estimating this Guardian thing,' said Martin optimistically. 'It may have created some disturbing phenomena, but it hasn't injured anyone yet. Not physically. Surely if it had that power it would already have used it?'

'That's what I thought,' said Terry, 'but Marion thinks otherwise. She says it will become progressively more dangerous.'

'Until what?' Martin asked.

Terry swallowed hard. 'Until it kills someone.'

Of course they did not say it, but that 'someone' seemed likely to be Terry Shotton.

Any hope they had drawn from the respite since 21st August was cruelly snatched away later that afternoon. Graham and Martin were preparing to leave when Terry suddenly went as white as a sheet. He stood in petrified silence as if desperately willing something to go away.

The two men stared at each other.

'What is it?' asked Graham.

Terry said nothing for a few seconds, then grimaced and looked at his friends. 'Can't you feel it?' he said imploringly.

'Feel what?' said Martin.

'The cold.' Terry rubbed his arms. 'It's back.'

It was a moment before they noticed it, then Pat felt it too, so did Terry's mother who had been sitting in the lounge watching television. Graham and Martin decided to stay, allowing Martin first hand experience of the icy, oppressive atmosphere that had settled over the Shotton home. For the next hour the distressing sensation continued to grow. A heavy melancholic depression that seemed to seep from the walls and into the very pores of their skin. They began to get mild static shocks if they touched metal objects and on a number of occasions the television screen went fuzzy and a loud crackling shook the speaker. The air felt electrically charged.

Just after 5.30 p.m. the two children arrived home, Neil took his bike to the garden shed and Joanne helped her mother with the dinner. They had just settled down to eat when Neil burst in through the back door.

'There's a horrible noise in the garden,' he said, breathlessly. He described it as a high pitched ringing sound.

Terry recoiled in horror as he realised what it was. Seconds later it came again, only now it was inside the house. First overhead, then in the hallway and finally from all around them in the dining room where they were.

It was the same dreadful noise that had come from the pool.

'Come on kids, outside,' Pat commanded the children, as calmly as possible. Without a word they obeyed, followed by Terry who helped his bewildered mother from the kitchen and into the yard. Martin stood fast, transfixed by a morbid curiosity to see what would happen next. But Graham grabbed him by the arm and dragged him through the door.

For sometime they stood outside. Neil took Terry to where he had first heard the noise. Joanne clung to Pat, trembling with fear, and Terry's mother demanded an explanation. Throughout, Graham and Martin frantically debated what to do.

At last they went back indoors where it was still and silent, but the chill atmosphere persisted. An unnatural cold, a frightful aura surrounding and permeating the cottage. Terry was stricken with fear. He knew the Guardian had returned.

\* \* \* \*

The medium sat in the darkened room staring across the mahogany table, the wrinkles on her elderly face made deeper by the glow of the tiny red bulb. Around the table sat five others in the awkward high backed chairs, waiting with baited breath. They were nervous, but eager for the proceedings to commence.

Joe Larosa did not really know what to make of the incredible events, but his interest in the paranormal had been awakened. Out of curiosity he had contacted a local spiritualist and been invited to one of her meetings. Although he had read about them it was the first time he had actually participated in a clairvoyant sitting. He felt uneasy there. No-one in the room apart from Joe knew anything about the strange events he had found himself inexorably drawn into.

The medium began to breathe more heavily and her head was lowering slowly. After a moments intense silence the old women took a sharp breath and looked up rapidly. Her eyes stared ahead as if focusing on something outside the room.

As she spoke her voice was deeper than before, her accent more refined, but he noticed that occasionally a slight hint of her local dialect intruded. The medium addressed one of the sitters and began to speak of a departed relation. The woman responded enthusiastically. It seemed that the medium had assumed the personality of a doctor who had died in the Great War. This was evidently her spirit guide. For the next ten minutes the medium continued to speak, sending greetings, supposedly from the great beyond. Every so often she gave a string of christian names, apparently loved ones wishing to have themselves remembered to the living.

Not particularly convinced by this demonstration of supposed spirit survival, Joe's attention was beginning to wander, until something odd happened. The medium cut off in mid sentence and trembled as if jolted by a sudden shock.

'Joseph.' She spoke in a quiet voice that betrayed surprise and deep concern. Her accent had returned, the 'Doctor' was gone. 'There is great danger.'

A shiver ran down his spine as he lowered a hand from his chin and sat up straight. 'There is someone here,' she gasped, staring over his shoulder. He turned nervously but saw nothing. 'A lady in white. She is warning you. She wants to speak.' They all stared at her in fear as the old woman's awestruck eyes opened wide with dread. 'Oh God,' she pleaded. 'No ... The power ... Please ... No!' With surprising agility she leaped from the chair and pulled back the curtains, drawing everyone back to the cold light of day.

'What was it?' implored Joe.

The medium stood by the window, trembling and shaking in numbed silence.

'Nothing,' she quivered, 'It's all over. Please leave.'

The old lady hurried them to the door and ushered them from the house.

\* \* \* \*

Pat had taken the children to Terry's mother's leaving the men to await the darkness. Just before 7.00 p.m. the telephone rang. It was Joe, and he breathlessly described what had happened to the medium, adding that he was sure it had been Gwevaraugh attempting to communicate.

Without hesitation Terry agreed that they must get together immediately. No-one liked the idea of staying in the cottage after dark and so they telephoned Marion, arranging to meet at her house. Martin, however, had to go home because his sister was ill.

As darkness fell Terry locked the door of his desecrated home and quickly drove away, not knowing if he would ever return.

# Chapter Twelve
# The Seance

**Transcript of the night's proceedings at the Sunderland's house dated 11 and 12 September 1982**

23.00 hrs (approx). Terry and Graham arrive and Marion telephones some of the others involved. They are either not in or live too far away to make the journey.

23.20 hrs. Joe arrives and the situation is discussed. Joe is sure Gwevaraugh wants to communicate, but Marion has no intention of attempting a trance. Terry suggests a ouija board instead. He thinks that by using the glass and letters Gwevaraugh could speak indirectly without anyone being harmed. Everyone agrees to try.

A pack of Lexicon cards are used and the letters A-Z arranged in a circle on the kitchen table. The words YES and NO are also written on two pieces of paper and placed in the circle.

An upturned wine-glass is positioned in the centre and the participants place their right index fingers on the base of the glass. If successful it should move to the various letters and spell out a message.

Present at the table: Terry, Joe, Graham, Fred, Gaynor and Marion.

Terry — Is there anyone there?
(No answer)
Terry — Does Gwevaraugh want to speak to us?
(Glass moves slightly)
Graham — If there is anyone who wishes to communicate with us can you please move the glass to YES?
(Nothing happens)
Marion — Is there anyone who can help us?
(Glass moves about three inches)
Terry — Please Gwevaraugh can you speak to us?
(Glass moves quickly to YES)
Marion — Gwevaraugh is that you?
(Glass moves in wide circle and back to YES)

| | |
|---|---|
| Graham — | Do you have a message for us?<br>**YES** |
| Marion — | Can you spell it out please?<br>**TESRY** |
| Marion — | Are you trying to spell 'Terry'?<br>(Glass moves quickly)<br>**Safe for now.** |
| Joe — | Did you try to give a message to P....? (name of medium withheld by request)<br>**YES** |
| Graham — | What's causing the strange happenings in Terry's house?<br>**Curse** |
| Graham — | Do you mean what we call the Guardian?<br>**YES** |
| Graham — | What is the Guardian?<br>**A thought** |
| Graham — | Do you mean a thought form?<br>(Glass moves to letters but makes no sense) |
| Graham — | Can you explain how it was created?<br>(No answer) |
| Marion — | Are you here to help us?<br>**YES** |
| Marion — | Can you spell out your message?<br>**I have had to wait.** |
| Marion — | Do you mean before you could tell us something?<br>**YES** |
| Graham — | Why?<br>**You will not understand.**<br>(Terry and Graham discuss what to do. Graham says he is concerned over one or two things and the others agree to let him ask the questions.) |
| Graham — | Are you still there?<br>**YES** |
| Graham — | Do you mind if I ask you a few questions?<br>**NO** |
| Graham — | Are you Gwevaraugh?<br>**YES** |
| Graham — | Are you the figure we saw in Dove Valley?<br>**YES** |
| Marion — | Did you speak to Nerys?<br>**YES** |
| Graham — | When did you live?<br>**Long time** |

Graham —   Do you mean a long time ago?
            **YES**
Graham —   Did you live in what we now call the Iron Age?
            (Glass moves to letters but makes no sense. Discussion
            between the participants about the best way to phrase
            the question.)
Graham —   Did you live more than two thousand years ago?
            (Glass moves in a circle.)
Graham —   How do you know our language?
            **I use your thoughts.**
Graham —   Do you know about The Eye of Fire?
            **Please let me tell you.**
            (Discussion between participants.)
Terry —    Please continue.
            **I know of the Stone. I am tied to its destiny.**
Marion —   Can you tell us in what way?
            **NO. Too long to tell.**
Terry —    Will the Red Stone stop the Guardian?
            **Once it is found the Guardian will cease to exist.**
Terry —    Can you tell us where it is?
            **It is not so simple**
Graham —   Did Mary Heath hide the Red Stone?
            **She did not hide it in the way you mean, but she did
            assure its safety.**
Terry —    How do we find it?
            **Only at certain times of the year can the Stone be
            retrieved.**
Terry —    Why?
            **It is far too difficult for me to explain. You must
            place your trust in me and I will help.**
Graham —   Could you appear to us now?
            **I can only do so at certain times.**
Terry —    When is the next time the Stone can be retrieved?
            **On September the nineteenth**
Marion —   Is that why you've had to wait until now to tell us?
            **Partly**
Terry —    What do we have to do?
            **I will explain what happened to the Eye of Fire.
            There is an old Abbey that stands on a site long
            revered as a place of power. Mary went to the
            abbey and left in its walls the knowledge of the
            Stones location.**
Graham —   Do you mean like a psychic tape recording?
            (Glass moves in a circle)

Graham — Do you know what a tape recorder is?
(No answer)

Graham — Can you explain how she did this?
**She used the power of The Eye of Fire to store her thoughts just as she used it to create the Guardian. Once she had prepared the way for its discovery and brought about the means of its protection she relieved herself of its possession.**

Marion — Do you mean she left the message and concealed the bell before she hid the Stone?
**YES**

Terry — Do you know where the Stone is?
**I know how it was placed beyond human grasp but I do not know the place**

Graham — But you know so much about Mary Heath. Is there no way you could tune in to where she put the Stone?
**I told you that my destiny was tied to the Red Stone, I therefore know much of its history as I do yours, for my destiny is also tied to the Green Stone that you already possess. I cannot know that which Mary Heath wished so strongly for no-one to know. Mary wished only one person to find The Eye of Fire.**

Marion — I think I understand, but does that mean you can't help us find it?
**I can tell you where to find the message she left. That will lead you to the Stone.**

Graham — You said the psychic message, or whatever it was, is in an abbey. Would that be Coombe or Ranton Abbey?
**NO. It is called Saint Bennet's Abbey**

Terry — Where's that?
**In the county of Norfolk.**

Graham — Is the Abbey called that today?
**YES**

Terry — If we go to this abbey will we be able to receive the psychic message?
**Only if you are there on September the nineteenth as the sun rises. If you are there at that time ring the bell and the knowledge she left will be yours. You will know where to go to retrieve The Eye of Fire.**

Graham — Did Mary Heath programme the psychic message to be triggered by the tone of the bell?

(Glass moves in a circle. This appears to indicate that she does not understand.)

Graham — Does the sound of the bell release the information Mary stored there?

**YES. As that was the intention of her thoughts at that time so it would always be.**

Graham — Does that mean she could have used anything to trigger off the message?

**YES. You are right.**

Graham — But did it have to be a sound?

**NO**

Graham — Then why did she decide on a bell?

**Lady B...** (Here the glass spelt out the name of the person for whom the message was intended in the 19th century but on request of the living descendants the name has been withheld) **would have known what the bell meant. She was very close to Mary Heath and knew the secret of the Order. She knew how the safety of the Stone could be secured if the need ever arose. What she did not know was where. When Mary knew her life to be in danger she knew that Lady B. was the only one she could trust who was unknown to her adversaries. The only one who would be safe. In the summer of the year that the Stone was concealed Lady B. left England to travel abroad. On their last meeting Mary told her that should anything fail before her return she would leave a message so that Lady B. would know from where to retrieve the Stone.**

(Marion complained of cramp in her arm and asked if everyone could rest for a few minutes before continuing. The glass moved to **YES**. The time 2.30 a.m.)

2.50 a.m. Fingers are again placed on the glass.

Marion — Are you still there?

**YES**

Graham — You said that Mary Heath told Lady B. that she would leave her a message. Is that right?

**YES**

Graham — Do you mean the psychic message?

**YES**

Graham — Did Lady B. know what kind of message it would be?

**YES. Mary told her. It had to be such a message to**

assure complete secrecy.

Graham — Please continue.

**At their last meeting even Mary herself did not know the exact place where the Stone would be secured. There were many locations that it could be done and many factors that would govern her choice. She told Lady B. that if this had to be done before her return she would leave something which would tell her where the message was, an indicator that only the two of them would understand. She would leave it in a pre-arranged hiding place at Ranton Abbey.**

Terry — Why didn't Mary leave the actual psychic information at Ranton Abbey?

**The knowledge had to be left near where the Stone was secured and Mary still did not know where that was to be.**

Graham — Why did the psychic message have to be near the Stone?

**Because the knowledge is not only a psychic message to locate the Stone, but also the power to call it forth.**

Terry — What do you mean by call it forth?

**I told you that the Stone is beyond human grasp. That is because it is shielded from the physical world by a force beyond understanding.**

Terry — Do you mean there's another Guardian?

**NO. The Stone does not exist in the physical plane, but it can be retrieved by calling upon it at the place where it was taken.**

Marion — Are you saying that it is outside time and space? (The glass moves in a circle).

Terry — Can you explain this? (Glass continues to move in a circle.)

Marion — Have we got this right? We must take the bell to St. Bennet's Abbey and ring it at sunrise on September the nineteenth. Then we will know where to go in order to find the Stone?

**YES**

Marion — Then we have to go to that place and call upon the Stone?

**YES**

Graham — When we call on the Stone do we just ask for it or what?

**The knowledge at St. Bennet's Abbey is also the knowledge of what to do.**

Terry — You haven't told us why Mary decided to use a bell as the means to trigger the psychic information.

**She could not risk leaving a written message at Ranton Abbey. Although unlikely, John Laing might have discovered it. It had to be something that only Lady B. would understand.**

Graham — Would Lady B. realise that she would have to ring the bell?

**YES. Mary told her it would be a sound that would release the knowledge.**

Terry — But how would the bell itself lead Lady B. to St. Bennet's Abbey?

**It was also a sign. Something she would recognise. A place they had visited together many times. They called it the Great Bell.**

Terry — What did they call the Great Bell?

**St. Bennet's Abbey**

Terry — Why?

**You will see**

Marion — So she knew where to go but did she know when?

**YES. As I told you she knew much of what Mary knew.**

Terry — Why if only Lady B. would know what the bell meant did Mary Heath have to create the Guardian to protect it?

**There was always a chance that John Laing would work out what it meant.**

Marion — Why didn't Mary safeguard the psychic knowledge itself to ensure that Laing could not obtain it?

**Such knowledge could not be protected in this way without the information itself being erased.**

**I must leave you now. Please tell me do you fully understand what you must do.**

(Marion repeats what has been said about St. Bennet's Abbey and the ringing of the bell there at sunrise on September 19th).

Terry — Where in the Abbey do we have to ring the bell?

**Within the Great Bell.**

Terry — Will we know where that is?

**YES**

Marion — You say that the Stone is somewhere near the Abbey. Do you know how near?

NO. But much of the land surrounding the Abbey is marsh and fenland only accessible by river. I believe the only way Mary could reach any possible location for the safe keeping of the Stone would have been by boat.

Terry — Do you mean we have to find a boat?

It will be your swiftest means of travel in that landscape. There are few roads and much impassable terrain. Your time will be short and a boat may be your best hope.

Terry — What do you mean our time will be short?

The creation you have called the Guardian grows in power all the time. Its attacks upon you will be stronger each time it returns. The time when the knowledge at the Great Bell is retrievable is also the time that the Guardian is at the height of its power, for it is also the time of the autumn equinox. You must retrieve the Stone by midnight on the nineteenth of September or the Guardian will materialize and destroy you.

Graham — What? All of us?

I do not know. But it will surely destroy the one who discovered the bell. I must leave you now. Remember you must be at Saint Bennet's Abbey at sunrise for once the time has passed your next chance could not be for many months.

Terry — What about the Guardian over the next week? Will I be safe?

You must hold fast.

Marion — Can't you help us?

Forgive me. I can do no more.

Marion — There are still many things we don't understand.

I have told you all I can. I must leave you now.

(The glass does not move again.)

Session ends at 5.17 a.m. Sunday 12th September 1982.

## Chapter Thirteen
# The Last Hope

There was only one week to go until the Sunday morning when they might at last discover The Eye of Fire, the Red Stone that would bring the terrifying ordeal to an end. All they had to do was be at St. Bennet's Abbey at sunrise on 19 September, ring the bell and the knowledge of its whereabouts would be theirs. They would then know where, and how to retrieve the Stone. No-one pretended to understand exactly what it was all about but now at least they knew what to do. With nothing further to go on they had to trust the seance message, it was their only hope.

The first priority was to locate St. Bennet's Abbey. 'Gwevaraugh' had told them that it was in Norfolk and still standing to this day. Graham returned to Coventry next morning and met up with Martin at Jean's house. They found the relevant Ordnance Survey maps and set about studying them grid by grid. At last they found it on Map 133 at Reference 384156. St. Bennet's Abbey was marked, standing just beside the River Bure about seven miles north-east of Norwich. They were relieved to find it was there.

They had been advised to acquire a boat, as the quickest and in many places only method of transport in this marshy district. Looking at the map they could see why. St. Bennet's Abbey stood at the heart of the Norfolk Broads, a low lying expanse of East Anglia where lakes and fens are connected by an arterial system of rivers, streams and canals. In many places the rivers widen to form the Broads themselves, large but often very shallow stretches of water formed centuries ago when ancient peat diggings became flooded. A tidal labyrinth of over 200 miles of navigable water. It is a fascinating area of study for the angler, yachtsman and canoeist but most of all a natural pleasure park for thousands of tourists, who each summer can hire the fleets of launches and cabin cruisers to explore the Broads.

They too must hire a boat from one of the many boat-yards in the district. The season was virtually over, so it might not be too difficult to hire a cabin cruiser for the weekend at such short notice.

First thing Monday morning Graham telephoned the tourist information office in Norwich and made enquiries. They put him on to the Hoseason's holiday company, who arranged a cabin cruiser for the following Saturday afternoon. Everything was ready. They would pick up the boat at 4.00 p.m. from one of the marinas at the small town of Wroxham, fortunately only about six miles upstream from the Abbey on the river Bure.

All they had to decide now was who would go. The boat would take a maximum of six people. Graham telephoned Terry and told him the news. It was obvious Terry had to be there, and of course Graham who had hired the boat, so now they needed four more.

Alan flatly refused. Mike was holidaying abroad and Marion was simply not up to it. No-one wanted to expose Gaynor to a possibly hazardous trip. Pat wanted to accompany Terry, but he refused to expose her to the potential dangers. Eventually they made up the numbers to six. Martin, Joe, Susan and Jean.

There were now only five days to wait, and still the Guardian had not returned.

* * * *

Two days after Terry had fled his home the Guardian came for him again. The children were still with his mother, but he had decided to return. Deep within his bones he knew it was useless to run. The Guardian was pursuing **him** not the cottage. Wherever he went it would seek him out, no matter where he chose to hide. Pat insisted she stay with him.

It began with a wailing cry from far across the fields, somewhere in the general direction of the pool. Terry was in the bathroom washing before going to bed. He heard the sound through the open window and his blood froze. He stood motionless in his dressing gown, hardly daring to move. He tried to believe it could be a fox. A completely rational explanation for the unearthly sound. But it came again, only this time nearer like the baying of a hungry wolf somewhere in the woods. All was quiet again as the seconds ticked by and Terry began to pray. Suddenly the fearsome screaming was close by, the vile rasp of an angry creature as it spat and snarled in the garden below. Then with the high pitched sound like a terrible ringing and an icy blast of wintry air, something invisible seemed to leap in through the bathroom window.

The net curtain flew back wildly, the lights dimmed and the shaving mirror misted over. The temperature dropped instantly to a bitter cold. Terry turned and tried to run from the room, but he tripped and crashed against the door slamming it shut. He was alone and yet something else was in the room, moving in the dark silence. His teeth chattered as he pulled himself up onto all fours. He could feel it bearing over him, a brooding black malevolence. He tried to crawl away, but was immobilised and vainly tried to scream as the laboured, embittered breathing began. He closed his eyes and waited, waited for what he felt was inevitable, that at any moment it would descend on him. But nothing happened. He felt cold water dripping on his face, it was condensation falling from the ceiling. But there was nothing else, in fact the room was becoming warm again. He opened his eyes and dragged himself to his feet just as Pat ran in.

* * * *

Everyone had hoped they would be free from the influence of the terrifying Guardian until the following Sunday, although the seance message had given them no such reassurance. Marion, however, now felt positive she knew what was occurring and what would happen.

They had been told the Guardian's influence would grow stronger each time it attacked, initially being able only to exert frightening psychic influence, but ultimately having the power to destroy its intended victim. It had been affected by their efforts at the pool, three weeks later it had returned, and now after only two more days, Terry had been assailed by it again. They were no longer able to fend it off. There was no means of protection available to them. Terry would simply have to endure each day, knowing that after it came there would be a time lapse before it struck again. Marion was certain that unopposed the Guardian would strike at Terry about once every 48 hours. Before Sunday morning it might attack at least twice more. Considering it would be increasingly dangerous each time, and judging by what had befallen Terry in his latest confrontation, Marion was convinced that he might not survive the week. She telephoned Graham.

'I don't see what we can do,' said Graham. 'Everything we try just seems to make it stronger.'

'I know,' said Marion despondently, 'but we must think of something, anything to give us time.'

Perhaps Marion was right. The Guardian had not appeared for three weeks after the episode at the pool. Even if it returned more powerfully after such a counter attack, they could perhaps knock it out long enough to get the Stone.

'You may be right,' said Graham, 'but we don't know what to do. We might make it so powerful it could destroy us all immediately.'

Marion thought for a moment. 'I suppose you're right. We did have a lucky escape at the pool, but we must think of something.' Graham agreed to try and work something out with Martin and Jean.

After some discussion Jean made an intriguing suggestion. 'Perhaps instead of attacking the Guardian you should try and befriend it.'

'I don't think it wants to be friends,' said Martin.

'Maybe not, but perhaps it would **have** to respond positively given the circumstances.'

'I don't understand.'

'The Guardian absorbs psychic energy and takes in what you throw at it, what if **that** happened to be friendship.'

Jean had a point. It was a long shot but it might just work. Perhaps if they projected friendly and benevolent emotions towards the Guardian it would respond likewise.

'If nothing else we might confuse it,' said Martin.

Although Graham and Martin agreed to try they had no idea how to summon the Guardian. It was Terry and Marion who had done it before. Bearing in mind her poor state of health it would be irresponsible to enlist Marion's help, and Terry was already in great danger, if he directly called upon the Guardian it might even kill him. Alternatively they could be with Terry when it attacked again, and try then, but it was more logical to try something immediately in case it failed and Terry was badly injured.

'What about going to Terry's house?' suggested Martin. 'The Guardian seems to have taken up residence there.'

'I don't think it has,' said Graham. 'Marion thinks the strange cold and oppressive atmosphere are a kind of psychic fallout, only a residue left by the Guardian.'

They must try and decide if the Guardian was always present when the chill depression descended, or whether Marion's 'fallout' theory was correct. Graham and Martin were on the brink of deciding to visit the cottage when Jean spoke.

'There might be another way,' she said, 'What about the bell itself?' Perhaps if they could concentrate on the bell they might communicate with the terrifying entity that was trying to destroy them.

* * * *

Wednesday, 14 September.

The small green bell was set in the middle of the table in Graham's back room as the two men each drew up a chair and prepared themselves.

They had no idea how or where to begin, but decided to spend a few moments consolidating their thoughts. They would think of the Guardian, concentrate on its reason for existing, and remember that they had been led to find it. They had after all done no wrong, but had simply followed Gaynor's psychic message. They had been directed to find the bell, and the Eye of Fire. They were not John Laing and they had not stolen the bell. Above all they must completely focus their minds on the one most important fact. Both they and the Guardian were on the same side.

Graham spoke first. 'Put your hands on the bell, think of the Guardian, and ask it to come.'

'Are you sure that's wise?' said Martin.

'No,' said Graham.

They laughed nervously, placed their hands on the bell and began to concentrate. A full five minutes later nothing had happened.

'Perhaps we ought to call it aloud,' suggested Martin. Graham nodded.

'Guardian, Guardian of the bell come to us now,' said Graham awkwardly.

Still nothing happened.

'Guardian. Please come to us,' Graham repeated.

Martin laughed, 'Perhaps it's busy frightening Terry,' he joked.

But his words were cut short. The bell suddenly began to vibrate on the table.

'What the hell ...?' Martin snatched his hands away and stared at the bell.

'It's working,' said Graham.

Martin hesitantly placed his hands back on the bell, suprised to feel it growing strangely warm to the touch.

'Guardian are you there?' Graham said.

The bell was growing hotter. A shrill note suddenly started to sound, not only from the bell but from all around the room as if the air itself was somehow responding to the hellish presence they both began to feel.

'Guardian we wish you no harm.' Graham's words sounded weird, a strange tinny echoing quality effected by the growing noise around them.

'We want to be ...! Aaaaagh!' They recoiled in pain as an electric shock jarred their arms from the bell itself.

'For Christ's sake,' yelled Martin. On and on went the continuous unbroken ringing that vibrated in their eardrums and set their teeth on edge.

Graham kicked away his chair and ran for the door. 'Let's go,' he cried.

Martin leapt up and followed, but a sudden freezing blast of air smashed him square in the face and blew him back hard against the wall.

Graham span round to see what had happened, but in an instant he too was flat on his back. The screaming note seemed to make the whole room vibrate as cups and plates shook from the sideboard and crashed to the floor. The room was bitterly cold and a fierce, electrifying wind was howling through the air. No windows or doors were open, but still it rushed in. Blast after icy blast, making their skin crawl and shiver. It pierced their eyes and dried their flesh. It was so strong that it was becoming impossible to breath.

'Guardian ... wha ... whatever you are ... we ...' Graham began to cough violently. Martin dragged himself across the floor to Graham as he retched and choked on the acrid air.

'We've got ... got to get out.' he spluttered, but his words were almost inaudible above the sickening shriek emanating from the bell and filling the room.

Together the breathless figures forced themselves to stand, not knowing or caring if it was the wind or a salvo of atmospheric vibrations that forced them back. A book, its pages open and flapping crazily, was lifted from the sideboard and smashed against the lampstand, bowling it over.

They managed to drag themselves up, and with their heads bowed against the wind and their arms shielding their faces they forced their way toward to door. Another angry blast hurled them back and they toppled over, taking the table with them as they fell.

Suddenly the wind droped as the bell hit the floor, the only sound now its metallic tinkling as it rolled along and clattered to a halt as it hit the wall.

## Chapter Fourteen
# The Nightcomer

Their last hope of quelling the vengeful Guardian was dashed. Graham and Martin were quite shaken, but apart from a few bruises, had not been badly hurt during their ordeal. There was nothing left for them to do. They would simply have to wait and see if Marion was right about the Guardian returning every 48 hours. There was a last, slight chance that the energy it expended in Graham's flat had rendered it powerless for a short time. Hopefully it would not come for Terry again on Wednesday night.

* * * *

Terry sat in the armchair, white faced and dark eyed. He was unshaven and tired. But he was resolved not to sleep, at least not yet. He would be all right after midnight he reckoned. If nothing had happened by then, he knew he would be safe for that night, at least that is what he hoped. The others had offered to stay with him but he had refused, that is apart from Pat who would not leave no matter how much he begged her; no-one should be exposed to the same danger that threatened him. It was not just that they might also be harmed, but he had to take account of Marion's belief that if others were with him the Guardian could become even stronger. It drained people of their life force, using it to power itself. If Terry was accompanied it would use them against him. So it seemed logical that he had a better chance alone, and their past experience led him to believe there was little anyone could do anyway.

It was just after 11.30 p.m. when the noise came. Terry turned down the television set, listening intently, every nerve on edge. There it was again, somewhere outside. Pat was upstairs, probably asleep. He hadn't told her Marion's theory and she therefore had no reason to believe the Guardian would return. He had told Pat that everything would be all right now that Graham and Martin had discharged the Guardian's power. He prayed he was right, but now he knew he was wrong. Once more it was coming for him, and this time it was more powerful than ever.

Quiet and trembling Terry made his way to the back door. He was determined to leave the cottage, walk out into the night and face the unearthly terror away from Pat so she would be safe. The cry came again from across the fields, from the same direction as before. He entered the dark garden and walked towards the sound.

He tried to tell himself it was only an illusion, a thought creation; surely it could do him no real harm, could not even exist unless he believed in it.

Like a death knell in the night the ringing came from the orchard at the end of his garden. His legs began to weaken and his heart started to pound. Now the breathing drew near, angry and hoarse, coming closer as he waited in anguished silence.

But nothing happened, the sounds stopped. He continued to the end of the garden and leant against the fence, screwing his eyes tightly shut and waiting. After what seemed like an eternity he looked around into the darkness. The infernal thing had gone. He wondered if perhaps by some miracle he had destroyed it. Facing it head on had perhaps robbed it of its power. He had defied it and overcome it. Yes, that must be it. He had faced his own living nightmare.

\* \* \* \*

Next day he spoke to Marion and told her what had happened. She listened sympathetically but did not tell him what she knew. That morning Gaynor had received a psychic impression. Because of what Graham and Martin had done with the bell the Guardian's power had been temporarily sapped, but now it would return with a vengeance.

Gaynor said that 19 September was now so near that all the Guardian's attention would be directed on Terry. Others who had tried to defeat it were now incidental to its programming, it was Terry, the man who had found the bell, that must be destroyed. On Friday night she felt sure the Guardian would return. Marion phoned Graham and gave him this news, hoping that something could be done to stop it's next attack.

Although Marion said there was no point, Graham and Martin decided to repeat their previous experiment with the bell. They were both scared, but resolved that something had to be done to help Terry. If he could only survive Friday night they would get to St. Bennet's Abbey and all would be well.

Graham and Martin reasoned that once the strange events began they could overturn the bell and the phenomena would cease - just as had happened before.

However, their plan failed. They called upon the Guardian and the ringing noise began, but it lasted only a few brief seconds before dying away. Nothing else occurred no matter how much they willed the Guardian to appear.

Still reluctant to give up hope, Graham and Martin in Coventry and Marion in North Wales tried desperately to think of something, anything, that would help. At last they had one final idea. It was to try and find a place of protection, like the pool, where they might somehow be able to raise the necessary power to waylay the Guardian for the last two days. The pool was no longer of any use. Whatever power it had was spent, and the Guardian already possessed an equal countering force. Although the power from the pool had been able to affect the Guardian, according to Gaynor it had also immunised it. If they could find another place, somewhere even stronger, then perhaps they could repeat the attempt to stall the Guardian. Everyone feared that Terry could not endure another attack, so although very risky and possibly highly dangerous it was at least another chance. A major problem remained, for no-one knew of such a place.

'What about Brinklow?' said Marion. 'The lady in Gaynor's vision rode there, perhaps she knew it was a place of protection.'

'I don't think so,' said Martin, 'She only rode past it on her way to the tower.'

Marion had to agree. 'Still,' she said, 'you all drew the place. Surely it must be important.'

Graham agreed. Jean had also said she thought they were overlooking something at Brinklow. She had visited it alone on several occasions and felt very odd as she had stood at the summit. One of the dead elm trees had been all but totally destroyed. When questioned, none of the local people knew anything about it, but it appeared to have been struck by lightning and cracked in two. Stranger still, next time she visited the hill one of the huge boughs, some fifteen feet long and three feet in diameter was halfway down the hill. Because of its immense size and awkward shape Jean could think of no way it could have got there, and there were no drag marks in the grass or soil. It would have taken more than five men to move it to where it was. Perhaps Jean was right, but Graham and Martin did not think it significant. However, as Jean had asked them to go across with her, they decided to take a look.

Having decided to visit Brinklow they invited David and Sheila Bavington to join them, since David had drawn the hill. They also tried to contact Mary Harrison, but she was unavailable.

As the five stood on the hill surveying the landscape that sunny mid-afternoon, Graham borrowed Jean's camera and took several photographs of the fallen tree and huge bow which Jean thought was unusually placed.

Without warning Sheila suddenly complained that she felt very strange. The same uneasy sensation she had felt before at Knight's Pool when they had witnessed the mysterious watcher figure.

'There's something here, something horrible.'

They all looked at her with dismay as she asked if they could leave. No-one else had received any kind of psychic impression or message, so with nothing further to be gained they left and returned to Coventry.

During the rest of Thursday and Friday, Graham, Martin and Marion vigorously discussed a number of other possibilities, but ultimately they were at a loss to find a way forward. Gaynor had no further inspiration and neither Joe not Jean had any suggestions to help Terry in his hour of need.

Late Friday afternoon Susan telephoned to arrange for Graham to pick her up from Coventry railway station when she arrived from London later that evening. She would spend the night at Jean's and they would all drive to Norfolk on Saturday, meeting up with Joe and Terry in the afternoon. They would then pick up the boat, sail down river to St. Bennet's Abbey and moor there for the night to be fully prepared for the sunrise on Sunday morning.

As dusk began to fall all they could do was wait for the morning and pray that Terry would be all right.

* * * *

The night was quiet, and Terry lay awake counting the minutes. The green illuminated numbers on the digital clock read 00.28. 12 o'clock had passed without event, but not the dreadful hour of 1 a.m., true midnight, by British summer time. In G.M.T. the clock should read 23.28. Still thirty two minutes away from the middle of the night. Why midnight was so important he had no idea. It was exactly halfway between sundown and sunrise, but what occult significance that might have he did not care to think. During the seance at Marion's they had been told that if they had not found the Stone by true midnight on Sunday 19th the Guardian would strike. It would materialise and destroy them. Good God, he thought, what did that mean? Terry was still confident that now they knew exactly what to do they **would** find the Stone. But as darkness closed about him his troubled thoughts once more returned to the Guardian. It was the next half hour that so frightened him. The Guardian was attacking near enough every 48 hours. He knew that once midnight had passed he would be safe. Over and over he told himself not to worry. He had faced the Guardian on Wednesday night and it had retreated. He had headed straight towards it and it had gone, perhaps for ever. Even if it still existed all he had to do was face it again. He lay awake waiting for the sound, the terrible haunting cry from across the fields. He would get out of bed, put on his coat and walk out into the night. He should really have been downstairs dressed and prepared, but Pat had insisted he join her in bed. She was tired and afraid. There was another reason too why he lay in bed; it gave him extra strength, helped him feel as if the Guardian could not break his daily routine. It was all part of the same logic that had helped him dissipate the Guardian two nights before.

Anyway, what did it matter if he faced it in his pyjamas and slippers, in fact perhaps it would help. It would show he was not afraid. And so the thoughts tossed and turned in his mind as he lay quietly in the light of the bedside lamp.

00.34. How the minutes dragged as he lay there waiting for a waking nightmare. His heart began to race as the noise came from away in the distance. But it was only a sheep bleating in the fields. 'Thank God,' he whispered, exhaling slowly.

Pat moved and turned over next to him still asleep and blissfully unaware of the disturbance. He kept hoping that he would fall asleep and suddenly wake up to find it light outside, the birds singing in the morning.

It happened suddenly. The room was plunged into darkness and Terry cried out in shock, fumbling for the light switch. He turned it ON ... OFF ... ON ... OFF. 'God. The bloody thing's fused.'

Even the illuminated digits of the clock had gone. For a second he thought he had been struck blind, until he caught a faint light filtering in through the curtains from the moonlight outside.

Pat was awakened by Terry's startled cry. 'What is it? ... Terry?'

'The light,' he whispered in the darkness, 'It just ...'

Icy cold flooded the room. At once the terrible laboured breathing was upon him, right in the room, at the end of the bed.

'Oh God ... Please ... no ...'

There had been no warning of its coming, no chance to prepare himself. Nothing.

The breathing grew louder, moving towards him up the bed. He tried to get away, break free and flee the room, but Pat was gripping him so tightly he could not move.

'Terry ... what's ...'

A sharp, sardonic hiss emanated as if through clenched and mocking teeth, like something in the darkness was grinning, delighting in his dread.

But he knew there could be nothing physical. It had no shape or form, no real substance. But perhaps he was wrong. He lay petrified in the darkness.

Panic overwhelmed him as he struggled again to free himself from Pat's vice-like grip.

'Let me get out. Please.'

'No,' she shouted, an inner strength suddenly coursing through her veins. 'It can't hurt us. It can't. Leave us!' She shouted, 'Leave us alone!'

A hideous rasping snarl came from the corner of the room, filling them with dread, it was a fading hiss of expired and fetid air.

Then Terry knew, almost as if it had told him itself, that the Guardian was gloating. It had come to strike fear into his very soul, but it could not destroy him until the appointed time. It was trying to drive him out of his mind with fear, but until the day when it was at the height of its power it could not fully materialise and defeat him.

As the sick hiss faded and merged with the night he thanked God he was safe. But now he knew with absolute conviction that they must find the Eye of Fire by midnight on Sunday. If they failed he was condemned to die.

\* \* \* \*

Terry had survived the final mind shaking assault and was safe until Sunday. They must find the Red Stone then. He hugged Pat and tried to sleep, but they both lay awake drifting on the edge of dreams.

Although he did not have to be in Wroxham until late Saturday afternoon Terry rose and phoned Joe well before sunrise. He could not stay in the cottage a moment longer. They would have to leave for Norfolk now. The sooner he reached the Broads the sooner he would feel safe. His new fear was that the Guardian might try and stop them getting there.

Kissing Pat goodbye he stepped out into the night and set off to collect Joe. At last they were on their way, escaping from the terrible nights of fear in the cottage and heading towards Wroxham in the early morning.

## Chapter Fifteen
# The Voyage

Susan had arrived in Coventry at about 10.30 p.m. on Friday evening and joined Graham and Martin at Jean's house. They told her about the frightening attacks which had been happening to Terry on alternate nights that week; the chill oppressive atmosphere, the strange unaccountable noises, and worst of all the terrifying disembodied breathing. Thankfully he hadn't telephoned to report anything that evening, so they could only assume that the assault had temporarily abated.

They had talked well into the night, wondering what would happen tomorrow and if new dangers lay ahead. They hoped they could find The Eye of Fire and lay the Guardian to rest forever. Terry's life depended on their success. He was hoping and praying for Saturday to arrive, to journey to Norfolk as soon as possible and face whatever lay ahead. Marion, too, was at her wit's end, hardly daring to sleep at night in case the Guardian returned. It was a dreadful strain on all of them. They could not help but admire Marion and Terry's courage over the last few weeks. It had been extremely difficult, but they had held fast against fear and uncertainty.

'I don't think Terry can hold out much longer,' said Graham, 'at least everything seems all right tonight.' He had no idea what Terry had gone through. Far away in Saverley Green Terry had experienced a night of living hell.

Considering the late hour at which they had gone to bed, everyone felt surprisingly refreshed and ready to face the day. Outside the morning sun shone brightly overhead and the blue sky was dotted with wisps of cloud. At least the weather looked good, it promised to be a fine day.

After lunch they left Coventry and set off towards Peterborough and East Anglia. The twisting roads wound their way across the landscape, which gradually became a wide, flat lowland as they drove eastwards. The road was agonisingly slow, too narrow and winding to safely overtake the heavy lorries forced to use it for lack of a motorway. Passing through Wisbech, Swaffham and East Dereham they at last came to Norwich and from there headed northeast along the A1151. It was now mid afternoon and the day was hot and sunny. They had arranged to meet Joe and Terry on the main roadbridge at Wroxham, a small town on the River Bure eight miles out of Norwich.

The place was alive with activity that fine, exhilerating day. Holidaying families, mischievious children with ice-cream speckled lips, and parties of youths setting out for a boisterous time on the Broads. At 4.00 p.m. they met up with Joe and Terry. Terry beamed at them as they approached, but beneath the veneer of unconcern they could sense something was deeply troubling him.

'Everything all right?' asked Martin, 'we assumed it was when you didn't phone.' Terry shook his head and recounted the horrific events of the night before. They listened with mounting concern as he related the gruesome details. 'I'm okay now,' he said, 'at least we've got a day's grace.' He smiled and leant over the bridge, surveying the waterway below.

Boats of all shapes and sizes chugged up and down the sparkling river. Middle aged men in 'popeye' hats, ludicrously trying to imitate sixteenth century buccaneers. The place was alive with the gentleness of an indian summer and sunshine.

Terry and Jean collected the boat and they were soon off, heading south-east towards ... towards what? For the first time that rapturously sunny day the awesome realisation of what might lie ahead dawned upon them. Would they be safe? What of the Guardian? Would it attack the boat? They hardly dared think.

'Full steam ahead,' cried Terry as he took the wheel. He was putting on a brave face. For a time they forgot their worries and soaked up the sun, which was still bright in the sky as they sailed along the river at a steady three knots.

Martin sat at the stern surveying the open landscape, passing vessels and the enchanting riverside houses. A boat passed by them and an attractive girl in her early twenties smiled invitingly. He smiled back and waved frivolously. 'Enjoy it while it lasts,' he thought.

It was growing steadily less warm as the sun slipped lower in the early evening sky. It had been a perfect summers' day; hot, dry and memorable. So far so good. In time they came to Horning and passed by a large riverside pub called the Old Ferry Inn. It was already busy, bustling with people drinking and eating. They sailed on, noticing that their boat was the only one now heading east. All others were making back for civilization, not away from it.

Soon they were in the very heart of the fenland. No houses to be seen, only river and marshland stretching away on either side. The sun was sinking low over the distant horizon and a cool breeze began to blow up from the water. Susan emerged from below deck carrying a tray of tea and coffee. Martin stood at the helm and looked up river. In the far distance a black silhouette stood out against the pale skyline. He fingered the map and looked again. That was it - they had found St. Bennet's Abbey.

He pointed eastwards, and almost in unison they looked towards it, a tall black tower beckoning them from afar. For a moment they all fell silent, watching and contemplating. It was 6.40 p.m. and as dusk approached they were becoming increasingly aware of the formidable task that lay ahead. Now they were within minutes of the Abbey, possibly their last few untroubled moments in the foreseeable future.

Terry slowed the boat and drew up against the riverbank. The engine coughed and died, bringing an uncanny silence to the twilight scene. Way back along the river they caught sight of a boat disappearing into the evening haze. The area was deserted, the cool waters lapping gently against the bows.

They made their way to the Abbey, which has been dated to the early ninth century, certainly from 1020, when King Cnut endowed it with three manors. By the medieval period it was large and spacious, 600 yards long and 350 yards wide across its broadest part. After the Dissolution the Abbey's religious function was usurped and it became a quarry site for local builders, then by the end of the eighteenth century most of the monastery buildings were destroyed. A windmill, used for crushing the oil from beans was built inside the ruined gatehouse.

The fine medieval walls and windmill loomed up before them, the grey stone walls towering overhead. The day was over and night was approaching fast, casting long shadows about the Abbey, giving an aura of timeless solitude. In an isolated spot, the building stands like a silent sentinel overlooking the marshy landscape.

Terry took a deep breath as he gazed up at the rough stonework. A chill wind brushed against him; it was growing colder by the minute now. He shook himself and stepped forward, the others quickly joining him inside the main windmill tower.

Gazing up at the lofty heights they wondered what the dawn might bring. For a time everyone was silent until Terry spoke.

'Well this is it.'

But no-one answered, they found the place disturbing. Its atmosphere was neither oppressive nor frightening, but somehow calm and unmoving. It emitted a feeling of serenity and solitude. Subjective or otherwise the sensation was intriguing and strangely settling, as if somehow they were safe within its walls.

Returning to the boat they sailed half a mile back up river and into the River Ant, mooring eventually at a place called Ant Mouth. They cast a final glance towards the Abbey then soon lost sight of it as darkness descended. Rather than stay in the boat and dwell on tomorrow's prospects Graham, Martin, Jean and Susan decided to make their way along the River Ant to a pub in Ludham Bridge about a mile away. Joe and Terry stayed behind on the boat to eat and rest.

Soon they were on the main road crossing the river and leading to the pub, its welcoming lights shining out to greet them as they approached, a familiar beacon in the night taking them away from the isolation of the river. Inside it was warm and noisy, buzzing with people and conversation, a lively mixture of holidaymakers and locals. The four of them tried hard to discuss lighter matters, but invariably the conversation strayed back to the task in hand. More than ever before it was unsettling, there were different elements; this time they were not on dry land, and the territory was new and unfamiliar, isolated and desolate. Although not too far from a large city they could not help feeling cut off. It seemed almost like another country, a land of rivers and lakes, marsh and swamp.

'Let's just hope Terry can hold on,' said Graham, 'it must be bloody awful knowing this thing's after you, and you alone.' Around 9.00 p.m. Graham left the others and made his way back along the dark riverbank. It was cold and clammy, made more strange by the surreal night-time landscape. Silver stars studded the pitch sky and a chill wind swept across from the marshes.

Up ahead he could just make out the boat and two black figures standing motionless on the bank next to it. Approaching cautiously and directing the beam of his torch forwards he found Terry and Joe staring fixedly in the direction of the Abbey.

'Look,' whispered Terry. Graham followed their line of vision and saw it immediately. A huge red star-like object hung directly over the building, casting an eerie red glow beneath it.

'What the hell's that?' exclaimed Graham.

'God knows,' said Joe, 'but its been there over five minutes.' The red light shimmered in the night, much larger and brighter than any star or planet. The three stood transfixed, staring in numbed silence at the mysterious object. Some sixty seconds later the light flared in brilliance and began to drop into the Abbey.

'Good grief,' said Joe, his mouth dropping open in amazement. The light descended slowly, and as it did so filled the building with a powerful red glow. A fiery luminescence pervaded the Abbey, throwing a deep blood red halo around the windmill tower and walls. The surrounding landscape was cloaked in darkness, but there only half a mile away was the Abbey bathed in the strange glow, suddenly and mysteriously illuminated by the vivid shining orb.

They stared in silence for several minutes as the deep red mist of light swirled around the building. Then, in the space of about twenty seconds, it faded, returning the Abbey to cold dark silence. They exchanged questioning glances. Joe spoke first. 'What the hell was that?'

Terry and Graham shrugged. 'I don't know,' said Terry, 'but something tells me we're in for a difficult time.' Somehow they wished Terry had not voiced the secret thought they all harboured. But they could feel it, a strange tension beginning to grow as if carried on the air itself. With a last glance towards the Abbey they clambered back on board the boat to await the return of the others.

Susan, Jean and Martin sat in the cabin listening attentively as Terry described the strange phenomenon at the Abbey.

'Then it faded and disappeared,' added Joe, as Terry concluded his account.

'Could it have been a flare?' asked Martin.

'Hardly,' said Terry, 'it was much too big.' After some discussion they opted to avoid the question of what the red orb could have been. All they could think was that it was in some way connected with, or indeed a manifestation of, the psychic information contained within the Abbey. Terry was becoming visibly more concerned as the night closed about their small boat. They should find out more, but could not think how. It was far too dangerous to attempt any form of trance, in such a state the Guardian might take over and possess one of them. The consequences of that did not bear thought, the damned thing would be on the boat, amongst them. They really needed to communicate with the information source 'Gwevaraugh' yet avoid the horrific prospect of possession.

Around 10.45 p.m. Joe made a suggestion. He thought perhaps they should attempt another seance, since it was the only way left to discover the answers they needed. They made up the letters of the alphabet and found a glass, and Martin agreed to take notes. After some minutes the glass began to move powerfully around the table.

Q.   Can you tell us what is going on?

A.   **Yes. You are safe until morning. When first light comes the Guardian will stir.**

Q.  How? We thought the Guardian was stronger at night?
A.  **It is now so powerful it makes no difference whether it is day or night.**
Q.  What about tonight? Will we be safe until dawn?
A.  **Sleep well tonight. You are protected, but tomorrow its strength will return and grow more powerful until midnight.**
Q.  What happens then?
A.  **If the Stone is not found by midnight the Guardian will materialize and destroy you.**

The glass moved no more. It was 11.02 p.m. 18 September, 1982.

Terry leant back from the table and took a deep breath. 'Well, that's it then. At least we're safe tonight.' They looked at him with concern. He seemed okay, not too disturbed by the seance message. Outside the wind had dropped over the river. It was cold but calm and the boat rocked gently on the waters.

Shortly after 11.45 p.m. they decided to retire. A long day lay ahead, and they would have to be up well before dawn. That night sleep came uneasily to all of them.

\* \* \* \*

Although temporarily assured of his safety Terry passed the night in fits and starts. He woke suddenly and unexpectedly, a transient dream phantom tugging at his mind. All around him it was deathly silent. He lay in the dark, alone with his thoughts. He had not said anything to the others, but he was absolutely terrified. It was like a living nightmare, he had the constant, unabating fear that at any moment the Guardian might attack again, descending upon him in the night. Theoretically he was safe until morning, but he was painfully aware of the gaping chasm that so often divides theory and practice. His mind would not rest. All he wanted was the night to pass and the welcoming light of morning to break. But the minutes passed like hours, dragging by with agonising slowness.

He looked at his watch. It was only 2.38 a.m. He turned over onto his stomach and tried to sleep, but it was no use, for Terry the night was like a great egg-timer, slowly but surely counting down to morning and first light. He finally pulled the sheets over his head and forced himself to sleep.

\* \* \* \*

Something stirred in the night. Jean shivered in her bunk and awoke. Turning onto her back she became aware of a new atmosphere on the boat, one of cold oppression and malevolence. As if the dark itself was watching, thousands of deep penetrating eyes surrounding and bearing down on her. The boat tremoured slightly, rocking on the water. She lay in the bunk, listening intently, her heart trembling. For a second the malevolence grew and passed through the boat, but then it was gone. Jean let out a sigh, realising suddenly that she had been holding her breath for nearly fifteen seconds. It was gone. But she knew this was only the beginning. The Guardian had probed the boat, unable to harm them, but at dawn there would be no stopping it. It would be a race against time to find the Stone and destroy the Guardian. Pushing it to the back of her mind she turned over and drifted back into troubled sleep.

* * * *

6.00 a.m. The alarm shrilled loud and clear, shattering the stillness and announcing the fated day. Struggling awake they dressed hurriedly in the chill of the morning. They were moored about half a mile from the Abbey so it should only be a fifteen minute journey to get there. They were quickly up and about, fighting off tiredness and trying desperately to get warm. It was a freezing morning. Patches of cold white mist swirled up from the river, saturating the damp grey landscape.

Martin rubbed his eyes and made his way on deck, clutching a mug of hot coffee. He shivered involuntarily and breathed sharply, the expelled air misting from his lips like icy smoke. He surveyed the chilly river, there was no-one in sight. Everyone in their right minds was still asleep and tucked up warmly in bed, not tired and freezing cold in the middle of nowhere at that ungodly hour. Turning south-east he looked towards the Abbey, now vaguely discernible in the distance.

Graham joined him on deck. 'Terry seems okay,' he said quietly. Martin nodded. Silently they looked at the others. Joe stretching his arms and then blowing into his cupped hands, while Jean, drawing her coat close about her, was smoking her first cigarette of the day. Graham and Martin exchanged a questioning glance. They hoped Jean and Joe would be up to it, after all, they were relative newcomers, and though Joe had witnessed the Gwevaraugh figure at Dovedale, it was only from a safe distance. Jean had experienced a vision of Coombe Abbey and been present at Dovedale, but nothing quite like this.

By now Terry was up on deck at the helm, peering downriver into the early morning gloom. The engine sputtered to life, churning up the river behind them and they were off, moving steadily downstream towards the River Bure and the Abbey. It was breezy and cold and they spoke little as the boat took them progressively closer to their destination. Time was getting on and it was beginning to grow lighter. Protesting moorhens scooted away from the approaching boat, its thick wake slapping against the banks. They reached the Bure and turned south-east into the wider channel, the minutes passing as the darkness faded into the dim grey light of early morning.

'Nearly there,' called Terry. The Abbey stood before them, set back a hundred yards or so from the bank. The scene was almost unreal, the air cold but strangely fresh. A thick carpet of white mist lay heavily over the Abbey, almost obscuring it, the windmill tower thrusting out ominously above the foggy haze below. Standing proud and silent against the sky, a bastion of stone and timelessness on the dew sodden landscape.

As Martin studied the black tower a revelation suddenly struck him. Of course, the tower was shaped like a huge bell, 'The Great Bell' as Mary Heath had called it. And then he remembered something, all those months ago, standing before Brinklow Hill, he had been sure then there was something they were overlooking, something staring them right in the face. For a brief moment the thought had flickered across his mind that the Hill was shaped like a great earthen bell. That was it, then, although the wrong location it had been the shape of a great bell, and that had been their final answer.

The icy fog swirled along the bank as they approached, pulling over to moor the boat before making for the Abbey. Martin turned as Joe gasped suddenly and pointed. A tall black figure stood motionless at the waters edge, drenched in swirling grey mist. A man in a long black coat. Martin scrutinised the figure for a moment before he realised what it was. He laughed aloud. 'It's a fisherman.' Concealed in the mist were half a dozen anglers, eager to make the most of the morning and avoid the disturbing swell of the boats that chase away their sport. But his laughter was short-lived. One of the men was clearly annoyed and stood up, gesturing violently.

'Sod off,' he shouted, 'you can't moor here.'

They suddenly became aware of the situation, mooring was forbidden at that time on Sunday mornings. An angling competition was in full swing and the anglers were by now so annoyed that a furious argument would likely ensure and someone might get hurt. Terry thrust the accelerator to full throttle and span the boat around, churning the waters like a wave machine, and washing them angrily against the bank. He was livid, cursing under his breath.

'I'll never eat bloody fish again,' he muttered, and straightening the boat raced back the way they had come. It was now 6.30 a.m. Time was growing agonisingly short and Terry knew it.

'We'll have to go back and try and make it overland,' he called. They nodded in agreement and urged him to make haste. After several minutes frantic searching they were back in the River Ant, where they at last found a short stretch of dry land against which to moor. Someone would have to stay with the boat, as there was nothing to tie up to.

'For God's sake go,' said Martin, 'I'll stay and look after it.' And with that they ran, racing as fast as they could towards the Abbey. Jean stayed to hold the second mooring rope, and the last thing she and Martin saw was their four friends disappearing from view into the trees.

'Oh God it's bloody hopeless,' cried Terry, as they realised their predicament. It was getting lighter all the time and between them and the Abbey was half a mile of swampland, a reedy impassable sump blocking their way. They stood overlooking it from a high dyke, searching desperately for a safe route.

'Over there,' said Joe, pointing towards what looked like a narrow pathway through the bog. Quickly they made their way along the grassy bank above the bulrushes and mud. It was now 6.43 a.m. and there was still time if they ran. Terry, however, suddenly stopped in mid flight and looked frantically about him.

'What was thaaaaa ......' Before he could finish what he was saying he was lifted from the bank and hurled down it like a rag doll. He rolled uncontrollably down the three yard dyke and sank feet first into the marsh.

* * * *

Terry had felt a sudden surge of fear as a black shape swooped from above and behind, a fast approaching shadow falling upon him. Suddenly his legs were kicked away and he was yanked into the air. His brain swirled in confusion and fear as the malevolence came like a tidal wave overtaking his mind. He was falling, tumbling painfully down the slope towards the muddy water. A sharp pain stabbed into the base of his spine as he span round and entered the quagmire.

He was in up to his knees and sinking fast, the oozing slime sucking at his feet, his face and head wet and cold while the force held his mind, pushing him downwards, deeper. Breathing awkwardly in sporadic deep gasps he fought to stay conscious and cry out for help. A desperate plea escaped his lips as the filth reached his waist, washing and surging around him as if driven by some elemental force. He clawed hopelessly at the bank, searching for a handhold, a root, a tree stump, or a thick handful of grass. But it was useless, he felt the icy water wash against his stomach as the black force thrust him still deeper into the foul mud beneath. Terror welled up and overtook him as he fought like a wild animal to gain a foothold. But there were no footholds in the mud. There was no chance, he was a dead man. The black tide swept over him and his mind went blank.

* * * *

'Quick!' screamed Susan, almost falling headfirst into the swell as she slithered down the bank to reach Terry. She flung herself at his outraised arms as he splashed desperately in the slimy morass, mud and water cascading over them from his frantic efforts to escape. By sheer good fortune their hands met and Susan fell backwards, pulling his limp body towards her. Terry coughed and spluttered violently, wretching as the oily mud seeped into the back of his throat. His eyes were wide by unseeing, filled with blind terror.

At that second Graham and Joe grabbed Susan and pulled her onto the bank, still clasping Terry's arms. They tumbled back up the slope, having saved Terry from what could undoubtedly have been a watery grave had they not been there to save him. They collapsed exhausted as Terry snorted mud from his mouth and nostrils. He was disoriented and confused, his eyes searching desperately to find something familiar. A brief flicker of recognition crossed his face as he focussed on the three of them. Then he sat bolt upright and stared at them hard in the eyes. For a second they feared for his sanity, but then he spoke with disturbing clarity and urgency.

'The Abbey, we must get to the Abbey ...' He stood up and raced along the bank towards the narrow path they had seen. They ran after him, mud and weeds spraying from Terry's filthy clothes and splattering over them as they caught up with him.

But it was too late. A crimson arc flickered on the distant skyline, a burnished shield of fire rising slowly from the earth. In seconds it spilled over the horizon, casting red shafts of light across the landscape, wiping away the pale shadows of morning.

'Shiiiiit!' screamed Terry. 'Run! Run!'

They raced like madmen towards the Abbey. It was now only two hundred yards away.

'Look,' shouted Terry. A misty red glow filled the windmill

tower, the psychic information they needed to find the stone. 'It's still there, it's still there,' he cried. But as they tore along the pathway and into the tower the glow faded and died away.

Gulping mouthfuls of air Terry held the bell aloft and struck it. The shrill tone rang out, filling the tower and echoing across the stones. Terry looked up and hit it again and again. The sound waves washed around the walls. But there was no response, they were too late.

Terry fell against the wall and slithered to the ground, tears streaming down his cheeks.

'No, no, no,' he repeated.

But 'no' it was.

## Chapter Sixteen
# The Eye of Fire

Far away in Flint, North Wales, Gaynor awoke to the sound of footsteps on the landing just outside her bedroom. Her younger sister Nerys slumbered peacefully on the lower bunk. She listened carefully, straining her ears towards any noise on the landing. There it was again, a heavy footfall on the floorboards. She was convinced something was out there, dark and unfeeling, watching and waiting for her.

The air was fraught with tension, an intense atmosphere of foreboding almost as if the house itself was aware of the intruder. Gaynor pulled back the bed covers very slowly and carefully twisted her legs round onto the bunk ladder. Step by cautious step she crept down and then stood, motionless, on the bedroom floor. Fighting desperately to breath even more quietly she took a tentative pace forward, edging her head around the corner of the door.

Her heart kicked at her chest and she stiffled a scream as she saw him. A tall dark Victorian figure in a long black coat. It was the ghost of John Laing only feet away, his cold penetrating eyes seeming to freeze her mind. She clenched her fists by her sides and retreated slowly back into the room, expecting him at any moment to stride forward and grab her by the throat.

He was coming! God no, he was coming for her! In a moment of utter desperation, she flung herself forward, hurtling through the door onto the landing. Better to fight than suffer the terrifying ordeal of waiting. Keeling forward she fell flat on her face on the landing carpet, only just managing to push her hands out and avoid a painful accident.

She lay on the floor, breathing rapidly and looking about in the early morning light. He was gone, but she was convinced now that he, too, sought the Stone.

* * * *

Terry was near breaking point, as he sat against the hard wall of the tower looking forlornly at his friends. His eyes were stained with tears, like two blood red balls sunk deep into their sockets. The desperate rush to make the Abbey on time and their failure to do so had completely demoralised him. Filthy and covered from head to foot in stinking mud he was utterly dejected. He snuffled and blew his nose.

'I'm finished,' he said, quietly. 'I can't take anymore.'

No-one knew what to say for the best. A misplaced word might wipe away any last vestige of hope in his mind. They stayed silent, praying he could pull himself together and find some last reserves of strength.

It was rapidly growing lighter, and slightly warmer as the new day filled the Abbey. A faint breeze brushed across the grass and birds sang merrily overhead. Ordinarily the scene would have been enchanting, but today was no ordinary day and now all it held was fear and uncertainty. Today promised to be the longest and most awful of their lives.

* * * *

Martin and Jean spoke little as they gripped the ropes holding the boat and paced along the river bank. They were wet and cold, able only to speculate on what might be happening to their friends, and the waiting was agonising.

Martin was deeply concerned, since the sun was up and still they had not returned. Jean stood motionless for a while on the bank, staring intently at the Abbey jutting out through the low-lying mist.

Just as Martin was about to set off to investigate, the others emerged through the trees on top of the dyke. Terry was covered from head to foot in mud.

'What happened!' implored Jean. Terry explained how he had been thrown into the swamp and overpowered by the Guardian. It had attacked and almost taken his life, and prevented him reaching the Abbey in time.

'Well. That's it,' concluded Terry, 'it's all over.'

'We can't give up,' said Graham, 'there might still be a chance.'

'I agree,' said Martin, 'Let's find somewhere to moor and all return to the Abbey. 'We might be safer there anyway.'

Terry swung the boat around and pointed it northwards up the River Ant. He was bloody scared, and he was aware his friends knew it. He dared not mention it but he could feel a strange disquieting atmosphere all about them. It grew stronger all the time, focussing around him and at the same time enveloping the boat. He wondered how long it would be before the Guardian came for him.

Below deck Jean and Susan were busy preparing a hearty breakfast, the smell of bacon drifting up on the cool misty breeze. Everyone was quiet, their thoughts with Terry and his dreadful predicament. He stood at the wheel, mustering a smile, but they knew it was forced.

Soon they reached Ludham Bridge and moored the boat. Constantly and painfully aware that time was short they wolfed the food down and made for the Abbey. It felt good to be back on dry land. At least with solid ground underfoot they could run if the need arose. The boat was like a floating tomb; if the Guardian attacked when they were in it there was no escape.

The sun was well up as they trudged along the main highway and turned right onto a minor road bordered by green hedgerows. Wide open fields and marshland stretched away for miles on both sides, dotted with occasional lines of trees, lonely farms and rickety swirling windmills.

In the pale morning light the landscape had a picture book quality, a feeling of unchanging serenity. But something else intruded on the scene, a hidden menace becoming steadily more aware of their passage across the fields. Terry wondered if the others could feel it.

He shook himself and looked up, he had lagged behind and broke into a quick trot as the others disappeared round the narrow cart track leading to the Abbey. The white mists cleared to reveal the isolated building about a mile away, the old ruin seemed to beckon invitingly, and they visibly quickened at their first sight of it.

By now they had all begun to sense the malaise. Occasional twinges of apprehension, a sudden urge to check nothing was behind them. It was a rather cheerless walk but their spirits lifted as they approached, surprised to find dozens of unoccupied cars at the end of the lane by the Abbey.

Terry cursed, realising the cars belonged to the anglers who had blocked their original approach and attempt to moor earlier in the day.

As he surveyed the building a glimmer of red light seemed to flare from a patch of stone quite near the top.

The Abbey stood silently before them, it appeared in the harsh light of day bleak and unmoving, as if aware of their plight but unable to disclose its secret. They filed into the windmill tower and stood huddled in the centre. Inside the air was cooler, the great circular walls blocking out the sun's warming rays. Although cold and gloomy, the age-old rocks closed about them almost reassuringly.

'Right. There must be something we can do,' said Martin, positively. Terry stared up at the tower walls and peered closely at the mossy bricks.

'I didn't mention it, but I keep seeing a red glow flaring from the walls of the tower. I think it might just be a sort of last remnant of the psychic information, like a fading echo.'

They nodded enthusiastically.

'Ring the bell again,' offered Joe, 'it can't do any harm. You might pick up some of the message.'

Terry held out the bell and struck it with his pen. The high tone resonated through the tower, all eyes focused on Terry's out-stretched arm. The bell rang out and for a moment stirred the tower to life. As it faded and died they looked questioningly at Terry; he said nothing, but again thrust out the bell and hit it, this time with much greater force. It rang once more, louder and more powerfully, as Terry screwed his eyes shut in desperate concentration. Soon the noise waned and drifted away.

Terry lowered his arm and opened his eyes. A deathly hush pervaded the tower as no-one dared speak, a fragile silence awaiting Terry's report.

He shrugged despondently. 'Nothing.'

'Nothing at all?' questioned Joe.

Terry shook his head. 'Just a fleeting image of a stretch of river. What else would you expect to see in this godforsaken place? It's nothing.'

He turned and walked quickly from the tower.

They all felt Terry was right, a stretch of river in the whole of the Norfolk Broads. It had to be an illusion of hope created by his mind in that forced moment of concentrated effort.

Terry stood outside the Abbey, alone with his thoughts. '**Damn this bloody thing**,' he muttered to himself, '**It hasn't beaten me yet**.' He refused to accept defeat. It seemed highly improbable that there was now any way forward, but he must remain optimistic and hopeful. He knew deep down it was up to **him** to find the Stone, but already the momentary image had faded into the back of his mind. With a final glance at the Abbey ruins he set off along the path back towards the boat.

The sun was climbing high in the clear blue sky, wiping away the last of the mists, as they approached their small cabin-cruiser at Ludham Bridge. Everyone was in surprisingly high spirits as the sun's welcoming glow invigorated their bodies and brought warmth to the scene; there was the boat perched on the river, rising and falling gently on the wash from passing boats. It was approaching noon and the riverside village was in full swing.

Everyone knew full well that a decision would soon have to be made. Only six or seven hours of daylight remained, leaving no time to sail around aimlessly trusting to luck that Terry received a psychic impression. He must make a decision right now.

Terry sat in the front cabin below deck, peering through a dirty porthole. A map of the broads lay open on the bunk beside him. He had studied it avidly, carefully searching for any hint of a location where the Stone might be. But the search had proved fruitless, leaving him thoroughly despondent and under enormous pressure.

He could not expect to make such a critical decision with nothing to go on.

Gulping the last of his tea he stepped out of the cabin to find the others waiting on deck.

'Which way?' asked Graham.

'God, I just don't know,' said Terry, 'I've literally no idea.' If he made the wrong choice there would be no going back. He glanced into the air, a distinct feeling of oppression had descended on the boat again, a chilling tension challenging him to decide.

'North.' The word almost fell from his lips to the deck. The agonising decision had been made, for better or worse, and Graham pulled the boat away from the bank. North it was, up the River Ant towards Barton Broad about three miles away. Although no-one cared to admit it they all felt relieved that Terry had decided, secretly hoping that his choice was somehow inspired.

Having settled that they should go up river Terry looked more than a little relieved. A great burden had been lifted from his shoulders, and for a time they forgot their fears and enjoyed the beautiful surroundings. The bright sun was riding high and the river cast a watery freshness into the mid-day air.

Terry stood at the wheel, scanning the muddy banks and gazing beyond into the high trees overhanging the river. There was nothing special, it all looked the same. The boat sailed on, hugging the bank and churning the peat-stained waters beneath.

Noon came and passed without event as once again Terry felt the sinking black malaise tightening its relentless grip around them, as if seeping into the very timbers and metal of the boat itself. The minutes turned to hours as still he searched, peering and craning his neck through the lush greenery along the banks.

In the far distance a shimmering blue radiance trembled above the horizon, a great lake stretching away as far as the eye could see. He glanced at the map, and identified it as Barton Broad.

Navigating the boat into the signposted channel they came onto the lake, a wide expanse dwarfing their small boat with its size. It was as if they had suddenly entered an inland sea. Although only a mile or so long and over half a mile wide the shallow lagoon seemed enormous compared to the narrow rivers which fed it.

Twenty minutes later they were safely through, still heading north up the Ant. Terry was growing restless. He had left the steering to Martin and was moving uneasily about the boat. Although it was still warm he felt strangely cold, occasionally shivering involuntarily.

'We must get to a phone. I need to speak to Marion,' he said.

A short time later Terry's wish was answered as they reached the next river town of Wayford Bridge. He leapt from the boat and raced to the telephone box, throwing the door open and grabbing the receiver.

Marion answered the telephone to hear Terry's anguished voice. 'Marion. We didn't get to the Abbey in time. What are we going to do?'

She told him about Gaynor's night-time confrontation with the dark watcher, and how Gaynor was convinced that he was the mysterious black magician John Laing. It was Laing who had shadowed their investigations throughout. She warned them that his restless spirit was searching for the Stone. Unfortunately she was at a loss to suggest any course of action. Terry replaced the receiver and slowly left the phone box, his face set and without emotion. The others followed disconsolately behind as he walked to the pub by the river and sat heavily on one of the benches.

'I give up,' he said, as they gathered round and sat down.

An air of complete despondency had descended. There seemed little point in continuing. They had no information to act on and Terry was completely resigned to his fate.

The sky was visibly darkening as black rain clouds scudded threateningly overhead. A cold breeze swept across from the river as the clouds opened up and a thick drizzling rain fell. Retreating to the marginally warmer interior of the pub they found a quiet corner.

'We can't just give up,' said Graham, half-heartedly.

'We can,' said Terry.

'And we have,' said Joe.

Graham looked at Martin who shrugged and shook his head as he glanced at the others. They had all thrown in the towel, Jean and Susan staring resignedly at their drinks.

'Well I'm not giving up,' said Graham defiantly. 'I'm going on up river until the bloody thing dries up. Anyone coming?'

No-one answered, but Graham downed his beer and strode from the pub, closely followed by Martin. The two stood outside, deliberating frantically.

'You'd better stay,' said Graham, 'keep their spirits up.' He laughed at his unintended pun. 'Get them drunk ... anything ... just keep them going.'

Martin nodded. 'Good luck.' And with that Graham turned and made for the boat, a tall grey figure hunched forward in the misty rain. Martin watched as the drizzle splashed on his face, he saw Graham jump on the boat and move away up river. Soon he was gone, lost from sight around a distant bend.

Martin looked through the rain spattered window of the pub at his four friends, silent and still in their small corner. He stepped back inside and bought a second pint.

\* \* \* \*

The black skies unleashed their heavy load on the bleak Norfolk landscape. Graham was drenched to the skin, squinting through the thick rain obscuring the narrow channel ahead. He felt nervous and unprotected. At least with everyone aboard there had been safety in numbers. Now he was alone, a single target on this mournful terrain. The map told him he was in Dilham Dyke, a mile long rivulet which ended at the village of the same name.

The sky was heavy and overcast as the cold rain poured relentlessly from above, pock marking the river and soaking the small boat.

Suddenly a thick judder rocked the boat, as if a giant foot had kicked the port side. He fell forward and clutched the wheel for support as the freezing wind seized the vessel. A black shape lurched from the bank across the bows and swept below deck.

The boat trembled and heaved as the dark form shook it back and forth on the water. Graham backed away. **The bloody thing's on the boat**.

A heavy slamming erupted from below as he was tossed backwards over the wheel. Cupboard and wardrobe doors smashing open and closed, the harsh banging echoing over the river.

Still the attack went on, a deep groaning and breathing, shaking the small boat with unmitigated fury. He could do nothing but seize the roof and hang on grimly as the Guardian tore through the vessel, shorting the electrical system and immobilising him in the narrow channel. He felt a sickening turn in his stomach as the monstrosity sucked all life from the boat and shot away on the icy wind.

Graham sank to the floor at the helm, head in hands, as the blood

152

pumped through his temples. His breath came in short, sharp, gasps, and his mind swirled in cold confusion. It took a full two minutes for his brain to settle and clear as the chill breeze bit severely at his face. Reaching up he grabbed the wheel and dragged his shaking body to its feet.

The Guardian was gone, the attack complete. The boat was totally immobilised by its frenzied attack. Try as he might Graham could not start the engine. Still the black sky poured scornful buckets on his bedraggled form as he struggled to bring the dead machinery back to life. This was it, a final destructive rage scuppering the boat miles from Terry; now their only means of transport was destroyed.

* * * *

Terry had sunk into an unrelenting depression. No matter what they said or did they could not shake him out of it. His hands trembled as he lifted his drink and took a nervous sip, his eyes wide and glistening. Even the cheery surroundings of the pub, fire blazing and busy with trade, did nothing to dispel his mounting terror.

In truth the others were more concerned for Terry's mental stability, and whether he could control his fear. If it got the better of him it might take over his mind and send him insane. It was too dreadful to contemplate, but these and other wild thoughts plagued their waiting minds. Sheets of rain washed against the pub windows as the minutes ticked by and half an hour later Graham had still not reappeared.

* * * *

The wind gusted steadily across the bows as Graham fought to start the boat. **Come on. Come on. For Christ's sake start**. The engine coughed and spluttered, refusing to respond to his frantic efforts. Overhead the threatening sky seemed to bear down upon him, defying him to continue. He was soaked to the skin and getting very cold, the biting wind clawing hungrily at his bones.

There was only one thing for it. Sit it out and hope the engine would miraculously recover. He slumped resignedly on the bunk and fell back against the hard wood. Overhead the grim skies grew ever darker.

* * * *

Terry stood in the pouring rain on the riverbank, staring fixedly at the water. He drew his coat about him and clutched his chest, stamping his feet against the cold. A glimmer of hope crossed his face as he turned and beckoned to the others frantically.

A familiar shape nosed slowly through the vaporous haze and moved towards them. At last, it was the boat.

BACK DOWN RIVER. The impression struck Terry with such force that he broke into a run and stumbled along the muddy bank. He never thought he would be pleased to see that claustrophobic little boat again. But there it was, a ray of hope on a wet and dirty landscape.

Terry leapt on deck and took the wheel as Graham quickly recounted the details of the Guardian's immobilising attack. It had taken him over ninety minutes to restart the engine and nurse it back down river. The bilge and water pump were out, but otherwise the boat was running just about normally. Everyone was aboard, enthusiastically discussing Terry's sudden and unexpected impression to head back down river.

It was their last hope. As if in uncaring confirmation the skies thundered open, unleashing a torrential downpour. Terry slammed open the throttle and surged the boat to full speed, standing defiantly at the helm like an obsessed and unswerving Captain Bligh. Never had they seen him so resolute and determined. The impression had filled him with new strength, at last he had been given an indication of the right direction.

The craft thundered downstream, weaving dangerously between other boats and their startled crews. Terry stormed on, his face set grimly and hardened with purpose. Still the rain cascaded in sheets, spraying across them on the turbulent eddies of air. Mile after furious mile they went until at last Terry relented and slowed the speeding vessel, a look of confusion spreading across his face.

His hands dropped from the wheel and he spoke for the first time since they had hared off from Wayford Bridge.

'That's it,' he said, pointing at the river and banks ahead. He had found it at last.

'Fantastic. That's brilliant. But which side?' asked Graham.

'That's just it, I don't know,' he answered, 'but this is definitely the place. I got a weird twinge across my forehead as we approached. For a split second the psychic image appeared and exactly overlaid this short stretch of river. Then I knew it was the right place.'

Graham nodded. 'But which side?' Terry shook his head as he realised he could not answer the most important question. He had found the right location, but was unable to say on which side of the river they should be. Darkness was approaching fast. The wind had dropped to a light breeze and the rain was now little more than an annoying drizzle. Terry looked from side to side, from one bank to the other, trying to recall the unconscious psychic image to help him. But it was no use, it would not return. He could only hope that it came back in a sudden flash as it had before. After some minutes the last light of grey day faded and he went below deck.

Everyone gathered around the small table in the main cabin. The light was gone, taken by the darkness and low hanging canopy of threatening rainclouds. A black night had descended.

Terry was beginning to look agitated. 'Perhaps we should try and contact Gwevaraugh,' suggested Joe. It was an idea, but a terrible risk if the Guardian came and possessed one of them. Attempting any form of trance was therefore out of the question, so it would have to be the ouija board again. A circle of letters was made and a glass upturned in the centre, but after ten minutes concentrated effort all they had was a lot of garbled nonsense.

Terry frowned and bit his lip. He felt trapped and helpless, as the hours were racing by and still they could not decide what to do. Everyone felt the strange tension gripping the tiny vessel, the tell-tale black malaise that heralded the arrival of the Guardian.

As time passed the situation was growing more desperate. They could not agree on a course of action acceptable to everyone. The day had gone by so slowly, allowing them too much time to think, calculate and worry. Now, when they needed time, the hours slipped by like minutes. It was past twelve with less than half an hour before the Guardian materialised.

'That's it,' said Terry, standing and making for the door. 'I'm going to get on the bank and ring the bell. It'll just have to be the correct bank.' As he stood up the boat suddenly rocked violently and a cold wind hissed into the room. Everyone felt it, the brooding malevolence watching. It was making ready, striking fear into their hearts before it came.

Terry ran through the door, up the steps and out onto the wet deck, the vague black silhouettes of night before him. Clutching the bell in his right hand he jumped onto the bank, sinking ankle deep in mud from the days rain. He cursed silently and looked at the sky. Cold white stars peeped through and appeared to move, an illusion caused by the clouds sweeping across the heavens.

Graham and Martin looked on from the boat as Terry held up the bell and hit it. The now distinct tone echoed out across the landscape and drifted off on the wind. There was silence, nothing happened. He rang it again but still nothing. Surely then it must be on the opposite bank. Martin and Graham glanced anxiously at one another and then back to Terry, eerily illuminated by his own torch.

What followed, happened in an instant. Terry called out that it had to be the opposite bank. An electric crack like shorting wires pierced the atmosphere as a massive sheet of intense blue light tore away the darkness just above the trees on the other side of the river. Terry threw a protective hand over his face and fell to his knees. Graham and Martin ducked for cover below the roof of the boat as the light flared in brilliance, flickered and then died, a wave of heat riding over them.

Terry cried out in agony. The agony of realisation. **'The Stone is on the opposite bank. So is the Guardian! Right on top of it! It knows we have nearly got the Stone and is concentrating all its power on stopping us reaching it before it materialises at midnight. If we want the Stone we'll have to go straight through it.'**

Although frightened out of his wits he at last knew his adversary. It was waiting, watching maliciously from the other bank, challenging him to come across and face it. The time had come, the hour of conflict, his own personal Armageddon. Fear pulsed through his veins as he stared across the river, the trees etched indistinctly between earth and sky.

He almost felt like diving into the freezing waters and swimming across towards the damned thing, dragging his soaking body out, ringing the bell and defying it. He might just have done it had a voice not suddenly called his name.

'Terry! Come on!' shouted Martin, 'Let's go.' The call stirred him into action. Pushing the bell into his coat pocket he staggered through the mud to the waiting boat. Martin and Graham reached over and pulled him aboard as it began to pour with rain.

Terry looked at them and said nothing. Rainwater dripped down his face and fell in droplets from his chin. No-one spoke; there was no need, there were just twelve minutes left before midnight.

Terry grabbed the wheel and started the engine, the muffled droning breaking the stillness of the night. Graham positioned himself at the stern, directing the powerful torchbeam at the propellor churned waters beneath. The white light shone over the river and panned across the trees like a roving searchlight.

Below deck the others stood rooted to the spot in nervous silence, a jumble of unclear thoughts running through their minds. But they had no time to think, for seconds later the boat was in the middle of the channel, rotating slowly and heading towards the opposite bank. They heard Graham's voice giving frantic directions to Terry at the helm. The torchbeam strobed across the trees as Graham sought a place to moor. Their blank, tense faces stared at one another as the realisation of what was happening finally hit them.

Weeks and months of psychic attacks on Marion and Terry and now this, the violent culmination and possible fatal showdown between Terry and the Guardian. It was too much, too hideous to contemplate. Still the rain splashed incessantly against the windows.

Moments later the boat shuddered to a grinding halt alongside the bank, throwing Joe against the table and winding him. Susan leant forward to help as Jean pulled him up by the shoulders. Martin made to go on deck when all hell let loose. A sick, throaty high-pitched, screaming wail rose above the trees and raced towards them. They froze in petrified silence, the furious onslaught of sound battering against their eardrums. A great swirling vortex of ice wind raged through the boat, tossing Martin backwards as he made for the door, crashing his head against the table and knocking him out cold. Graham pitched headfirst down the stairs and collapsed on the floor, almost crushing Martin's prone body. On deck Terry closed his eyes involuntarily in horror, their lids clenching rapidly in uncontrollable spasms.

'Ring the bell,' screamed Susan, 'ring the bell.' Her frantic cry broke through Terry's horror. Pulling the bell from his pocket he held it above his head and rang it furiously, crying out above the awful sound.

'I have come for the Stone. I have come for the Stone. I have come for the Stone.'

Graham clawed his way up the stairs as Jean and Susan hauled Martin's unconscious body into the front cabin and lifted him with difficulty onto one of the bunks. He was out cold but still breathing.

'Good God!' Joe's voice gasped the words with horror and amazement. Through the rain washed porthole a powerful crimson glow flashed and then hovered in the trees, a distinct red haze could be seen through the watery glass.

Still the wind howled and raged, shaking the boat with unbelievable ferocity. By now Graham was on deck with Terry, both men clinging to the roof for support as the boat rolled and tossed like a matchstick on the surging waters. The Guardian was upon them, screaming and wailing on the wind, diving down on the waves of rippling air as it began to take form. Five minutes to midnight.

It stopped without warning, a hypnotic calm taking over and everything around became a void. In the dark there was no rain, no wind, just a razor sharp silence. Time seemed to stand still as a high pitched airy hiss came from the red glowing mass in the trees, shimmering and pulsating less than fifteen feet away and only twelve feet above the earth. Graham and Terry stood transfixed, gazing in awe at the incredible sight. Terry stared through the darkness, eyes wide, while Graham stood aghast, looking on in amazement. Still the light remained, flickering in dazzling radiance before their eyes.

The hiss rose quickly to a louder higher pitch and expired with a great crack. In the unnatural silence the six foot ball of fire began a slow, measured descent. A deep crimson red sphere dropping slowly to the earth, focussing and contracting into a smaller fiery globe as it drifted down.

Terry was rooted to the spot, a sickly, black, sweet-tasting nausea hit his mind and throat. The Guardian ripped at his head in a last feverish attack. It felt like his brain was washing crazily in its cerebral fluid, swirling him in uncontrollable confusion as if dragged from its moorings. Through the painful haze he could just distinguish the Stone, within a blood red sphere the size of a tennis ball alighting on the grass only ten feet away. He struggled desperately to move, to stave off the agony ripping at his head and face. But it was hopeless, he could not move a muscle. With a last almighty effort he forced his mind to life and activated his voice.

'Graham,' he screamed, 'get it for Gods sake. Get the Stone! I'm dying!'

It was their last chance. Graham leapt from the boat and stumbled forward across the mud and wet grassy tufts. He watched in absolute amazement as the red ball condensed suddenly into a small hemisphere, a glowing luminescent red Stone on the black earth. He reached down and grabbed it, recoiling in pain as it burnt his fingers. He screamed in pain and dropped the red hot Stone.

Terry felt the seething monstrosity release his head and fire off towards Graham. It knew he had almost got the Stone. Terry staggered below deck, crying out to the others for help.

'It's got Graham, it'll kill him.' Tears streamed down his anguished face as a tumultous roaring power seized the boat and pushed it deeper into the water.

Graham cried out as the demonic force kicked the back of his head. He was catapulted forward, a single determined thought holding his mind together as the Guardian began to materialise on his head and shoulders. **Grab the Stone. Grab it. Hold it**. His skull began to give under the enormous pressure, a violent crushing force like two great hands pushing his temples in on his brain. A sick wave of pain swilled across his eyes as he almost lost sight of the Stone.

The others shot up on deck to see Graham on his knees in the mud, screaming in agony and clawing helplessly at the swirling vortex raging and materialising about his head and shoulders.

A great blue white glow appeared suddenly over the boat, a heavy cloud enveloping the vessel, punching it again still deeper in the water.

'Get back, get back,' cried Terry. They stumbled below deck as the Guardian's power soared to a feverish climax, attacking Graham and the boat simultaneously. Martin still lay unconscious in the cabin as they staggered below deck in terrified confusion.

Quite suddenly it was all over. Outside Graham screamed and fell silent. The dreadful wail dropped away and dispersed on the wind into the night. Then all was deathly silence as those inside stood rooted to the deck, waiting for something to happen.

The boat rocked slightly as something climbed aboard. Heavy thudding footsteps pounded across the boat, approaching like a nightmare down the wooden stairs towards them. They waited in absolute terror, waited for the materialized Guardian to enter the boat and destroy them all. From out of the darkness a tall figure moved slowly into the room and stood ominous and silent before them.

They heaved a sigh of relief. It was Graham. He held out his fist and unclenched his hand. On his palm was a small red Stone.

The Eye of Fire.

## Chapter Seventeen
# Lady of Light

The nightmare was over. Terry had survived and the Guardian was laid to rest. They had found The Eye of Fire. The small hemispherical Red Stone, an inch long and half an inch wide, had formed miraculously from a huge red ball of light. How, by any stretch of the imagination, this remarkable event had occurred remained a matter for pure speculation.

But who, or what, the dark watcher figure was they did not actually know. According to Gaynor it was the ghost of the Victorian occultist John Laing, who had also been trying to possess the Red Stone. His restless spirit driven on even after death in search of The Eye of Fire. Perhaps, however, Laing was merely a thought form unwittingly created by Mary Heath since it was he she most feared. Whatever the truth about the figure in the top hat and frock coat perhaps, like the Guardian, he had ceased to exist once the Stone was discovered.

Although the dark figure was not seen again after the Stone was found, on Thursday 23 September something else extraordinary occurred. Jean had collected the photographs taken on the Norfolk Broads, which included the roll of film used for the snaps of Brinklow Hill on 16 September. As she and Graham flicked through the monochrome prints they suddenly noticed something that should not have been there. On the picture of the huge bough lying half way down the slope was the unmistakeable figure of a man. A tall, black, silhouetted figure dressed in what appeared to be a Victorian frock coat and a top hat.

The unexpected image was also on the negative. It was solid, and it was definitely there, but how, they could not explain. A camera cannot photograph something that is not present or the eye cannot see, and nothing had been seen that day.

As the picture had been taken Jean and Sheila were standing just behind Graham. They had seen no-one, and furthermore David and Martin had been standing at the top of the hill less than two yards from the spot, and they, too, had seen nobody there. It was absolutely impossible for it to have been someone else on the hill that afternoon. No-one could have stood so close to David and Martin without being observed, but more pertinently Graham would have seen them in the viewfinder, and he had not.

They recalled how Sheila Bavington had felt a disturbing and malevolent presence there about the time the photograph was being taken, the same feeling she had experienced when they had all seen the dark watcher on Knight's Hill. It seemed just possible that the same figure, the same dark watcher they had inexplicably captured on film that afternoon on Brinklow Hill, was the figure they had come to think of as the ghost of John Laing.

But the most important question of all still remained. What was to be done with The Eye of Fire.

The following weekend everyone who had been involved met together at Terry's cottage, once more a peaceful place tucked away in its tranquil village setting in the heart of rural Staffordshire. It was almost as if nothing had happened, but the bell and the Red Stone in Terry's possession confirmed that it had.

Immediately after the Stone was found Marion's health improved dramatically, and within two days she had recovered completely. She was now convinced they would receive some psychic message telling them what to do next. But nothing at all occurred, even Gaynor had no answer.

'We'll have to wait and see,' was all she would say.

Everyone waited anxiously for some indication, or instruction as to their next course of action, but the days and weeks passed without event or psychic message. That is until Sunday 28 November.

Terry was in the living-room of his cottage, it was dark and late and he was preparing for bed. Upstairs Pat was in the bathroom and the two children were fast asleep.

He noticed it as he passed the back window on his way to the kitchen, a deep-blue light streaming in through the cracks in the heavy velvet curtains. For a second he thought it was car headlamps, someone driving up to the cottage. But the light was stationery. He thought perhaps someone had lost their way, accidentally having driven down the muddy lane which ended at his house, and they had stopped to look at the map.

He stood listening for the sound of a car engine ticking over, but all was quiet. Leaning forward he slowly drew back the curtain, peering out into the cold, dark night. Outside the lane runs on for ten yards to the last house in the village. On the other side of the track is Terry's private land, a long garden ending in a small apple orchard.

The steady blue light hung over the end of the orchard, not in the lane at all as he had first thought. He squinted through the glass, unable to make out the exact source through the trees. The light was a strange electric blue, unlike that of a torch or spotlight.

Terry was baffled, and he felt nervous and apprehensive after the terrible events that had plagued his home. He knew the Guardian was gone, but a blue light had often accompanied its presence, and it was impossible to dismiss the chilling memory of its attacks. He shook himself and became resolved to investigate.

Stepping out into the garden he saw the light hovering over the corner of the orchard. It was bright but not uncomfortable to the eye, a soft shade of blue holding constant in the night. He stepped sideways for a clearer view and stood amazed. A huge sphere of light hung motionless over the fence where the orchard meets the surrounding fields. It hovered silently ten feet above the ground, partly obscured at the left side by the apple trees.

Terry raced indoors to fetch Pat, but on their return the ball of light had disappeared.

* * * *

Although the grassy area was carefully investigated the following morning, nothing was found to account for the remarkable phenomenon. The local farmer was contacted to check if he had been doing anything unusual the previous night, but he had not, and he could think of nothing to explain the incident.

It was almost a month before the strange light was seen again, but on this occasion the event was much more dramatic. It was Sunday 12 December and Terry was holding a dinner party. Mike, Alan, Graham and Joe were amongst the guests. Alan had just arrived and come through the front door.

'There's a weird light in the garden,' he said, nervously. Terry had not told Alan of the most recent incident in case he misconstrued it. Alan was happy to visit the cottage once more now he thought the events associated with the Guardian were all over. He felt safe and secure again, but Terry considered it would not take much to frighten him away. Graham, however, knew about the appearance of the strange light and immediately headed into the dark garden to investigate.

'Get Terry,' shouted Graham. As he reached the garden he could hardly believe his eyes. About forty yards away, amongst the trees at the corner of the orchard, was a bright-blue orb of light bobbing up and down beside the fence. It looked about six feet in diameter and shimmered slightly around its periphery and it was quite silent.

As Graham began to walk towards it, the sphere rose into the air and drifted away slowly across the field.

At that moment Terry ran around the side of the cottage, closely followed by Joe, Mike, Alan and another guest, Janet Morgan.

'What the hell is that?' said Janet. By now the light was rising gently into the air and moving away slowly across the field like a great shivering balloon. But it could not have been carried by the wind, since it rose up and down, as if bouncing on an unseen cushion of air. They looked on in stunned silence as the light reached the other side of the meadow and took off into the sky, rising higher and higher until it was just a pinpoint of light over the distant horizon.

They walked a little apprehensively into the garden and made their way down to the orchard. The wind blew as they approached the area over which the light had hovered when Terry suddenly stopped.

'Look,' he said, pointing to the ground about ten feet away. On the damp grass, in front of an old yew tree, was an eerie misty blue glow. They moved towards it with caution, hunching forward and peering closely at the strange carpet of blue light. As they came closer they saw that it originated from a mass of luminous blue threads, like a great spiders web glowing in the dark about six feet in diameter.

The glow was slowly fading as they arrived at the spot and Terry hurried back to the house to fetch a torch. On his return the beam revealed a jumble of fine, webb-like threads which were no longer luminous. Terry flicked off the torch to check if the strange substance would react to light and glow again, but it did not.

Mike touched them first, gingerly pushing an index finger into the web. The hundreds of delicate strands looked like fine yarns of silk, so fine that they fell apart and seemed to evaporate into thin air when lifted.

Mike carefully scooped up a handful and took it back into the house. Within fifteen minutes the strange web in the garden had disappeared. Unfortunately, so too had the samples they had taken indoors.

* * * *

They were mystified by the strange blue light's return to the same spot in Terry's orchard. Some days later Terry saw an old map of Saverley Green, and he was surprised to find that where his orchard met the surrounding fields there had once been an old well. To his astonishment the well had been in the exact same spot over which the light had appeared, just by the old yew tree.

He informed Graham, who suggested Terry dig in the area to see if something was buried there. If nothing else it would be interesting to see if anything unusual was found which might help explain the strange light and web-like substance.

Terry agreed, and together he and Graham dug a five foot deep hole. They found nothing, but eventually reached the water table and the hole quickly filled with water.

Soon after Gaynor told them that in the time of the ancient celts, the time in which Gwevaraugh lived, certain wells were considered magical. It was believed that supernatural beings appeared at these sacred sites. By a strange twist of fate they had redug the original well, once called The Well of Sacred Blood. Now they must wait, and see if the light would return, but Gaynor could offer no further explanation. Terry enclosed the newly dug well with a small brick wall and they all waited to see what would happen next.

* * * *

Twelve months passed without further incident until on 12 December, exactly a year to the day after the ball of light last appeared, Gaynor announced that as many people as possible who had been involved in the search for The Eye of Fire must assemble at Terry's house.

It was short notice and only a handful of them could make it. Just after 8.00 p.m. that Monday evening Gaynor ushered Terry, Pat, Alan, Mike and Graham into the garden. It was a cold and crisp December night. Everyone stood mystified as Gaynor told them to wait.

She turned to Terry and asked him for the Stone he had guarded so closely all that year. During that time he had no idea what was to be done with it, but it had never left his possession. As he handed it to Gaynor that cloudy evening he felt strangely sad, as if somehow a final chapter was about to be concluded in their strange quest. Gaynor smiled and clasped his hand.

'Don't worry, it's the way it should be,' she said quietly, and with those enigmatic words turned and walked slowly down the garden path.

'Stay there, all of you. Whatever you do stay exactly where you are.'

They stood in silence as Gaynor disappeared into the darkness towards the well at the end of the orchard. A faint mist hung over the ground as they watched and waited, all eyes resting upon the shadowy form of the old yew that overhung the well less than thirty yards away. They knew Gaynor was there, but were unable to see her in the darkness.

Quite suddenly something began to happen. Away in the distance a pinpoint of light began to grow and approached across the fields towards the orchard. It was the same six-foot-diameter, blue sphere glowing softly around its edge. It dipped and slowed to a halt by the yew tree, hovering only inches above the mist covered grass in front of Gaynor. She stood out in dark silhouette against the ball of light, which pulsated and grew in brilliance with each passing second.

They gasped in absolute amazement as something began to appear from within the light, a human figure, white and dazzling. A woman in shimmering robes, arms outstretched and palms upturned in a gesture of peace. They gazed in awe as Gaynor stretched out her right hand towards the figure. The woman responded and leant forward slightly, and for a second their hands met.

The scene was quite fantastic, incredible, something they would never forget as long as they lived. The wonderful radiant being and the sixteen year old schoolgirl standing in fiery, mist-tinged illumination. It was a vision, a miracle, a picture of beauty that should last forever.

Suddenly the light flared in glowing brilliance, turned blood red and disappeared completely. The five onlookers stood in complete amazement as the seconds ticked by, the flaring after image of the almost blinding light still shimmering on the backs of their eyes.

Gaynor came back to them from the misty darkness and walked directly to Terry.

'The power of the Stone has been taken,' she said, 'it is not for us.'

'Who was she?' asked Graham, his voice unsteady, 'Gwevaraugh?'

Gaynor smiled as she answered. 'Whoever we want her to be.'